# The Dream Makers

# THE DREAM MAKERS:
## Discovering Your
## Breakthrough Dreams

### by
### RICHARD CORRIERE, Ph.D.,
### and
### JOSEPH HART, Ph.D.

FUNK & WAGNALLS
New York

Designed by Joy Chu

Manufactured in the United States of America

Library of Congress Cataloging in Publication Data

Corriere, Richard.
The dream makers.

Bibliography: p.
Includes index.
1. Dreams.   I. Hart, Joseph Truman, 1937–
joint author.   II. Title.
BF1091.C66      154.6′3      76-47680
ISBN 0-308-10276-2

1   3   5   7   9   10   8   6   4   2

*We dedicate this book to our friends,*
*who are in our lives and in our dreams.*
*We especially thank Konni and Gina*
*and Kedra and Signe and Steve*
*and Carole and Dominic and Lee and Leslie*
*and Jerry and Dana and Werner and Laurie*
*and Paul S. and Patty and Alan V.*
*and Michael G. and Don and Paul R. and Nina*
*and George and Inez and Nancy*
*and Alan S. and Vicki and John.*

# Contents

Introduction                          1

## Part One:
## The Dream Maker
## Tradition

1 The Breakthru Dream            7

## Part Two:
## Discovering the
## Dream Maker

2 The Dream Maker Visits      17
3 The Dream Maker Stays       34
4 More Dreams                 46
5 "Go Easy"                   54
6 More Dream Makers           65
7 "What's So Different and
   What's So New?"            76

Part Three:
Twenty-one Days to
Breakthru Dreaming—
How to Make Your
Dreams Work for You
(and Not Against You)

8 Learning How to
Remember Your
Dreams 87
9 Becoming a Dream
Maker: Week One 91
10 Becoming a Dream
Maker: Week Two 103
11 Becoming a Dream
Maker: Week Three 118

Part Four:
Applying
the Discovery—
A Dream Maker
Workshop

12 Who Is the Dream
Maker? 129
13 The What, Why, and
How of Dreaming 145
14 New Kinds of Dreams 170
15 After the Workshop 183

Appendixes:
What More
You Can Do

APPENDIX A:
Information about the
Center Foundation
and The Center for
Feeling Therapy 189
APPENDIX B:
Information about a
Variety of Dream Maker
Programs 194

. References and
Recommended
Reading                                          201
Index                                            207

# Introduction

In this book we tell you what we believe to be one of the most important psychological discoveries ever made—the Breakthru Dream. This kind of dream provides a natural way for people to give and get the help they need in their lives. We call this new way the Dream Maker Approach, helping people not only with old problems but also with new possibilities.

*The Dream Makers* is written both to tell a story and to teach "how-tos." The book tells the story of how we discovered Breakthru Dreams, yet it is not a novel because it describes real happenings. We are not novelists; we are therapists and our basic skill is in helping people change their lives. We know that there is a critical shortage of good doctors and it is our hope that the teachings in this book will allow many people to help themselves with their emotional difficulties. We know that the Dream Maker Approach can lead people to create a more sane, more liveable world for themselves, even when faced with the problems of living in this hectic, fast-paced world.

Although the Breakthru Dream and the Dream Maker Approach were discoveries for us (and for modern psychology), they were also rediscoveries of something that has been going on since the beginnings of human culture. The Dream Maker Tradition is a way of self-help and group change which has existed since prehistoric times. Here and there in the book we will tell you about some of your Dream Maker ancestors.

## Four Basic Ideas

Throughout the book we will emphasize four basic ideas so that by the time you finish reading you will be completely familiar with them. This familiarity will help you understand what is happening when your own dreams begin to change.

The first idea (and discovery) is that of the *Breakthru Dream,* which is a "snapping" between the conscious and unconscious mind; an eruption. When it first comes to you it feels like the longest nightmare you have ever experienced, but by the time it is over you've been changed. It becomes a "daymare" because it does not pass with waking. The Breakthru Dream occurs naturally but most people are afraid of it. We will teach you how to keep it and use it to your advantage.

The second idea is that *Breakthru Dreams have consequences.* Once you begin having these dreams you will develop a new awareness. We call it Dream Maker Awareness. The closest resemblance to this new awareness is Satori, or a good LSD trip, or a peak experience. Dream Maker Awareness combines the emotional power of the unconscious with heightened control and understanding by the conscious mind.

The third idea is that of the *Dream Maker Process.* This is the primary process which allows you to have Breakthru Dreams. (We have used the untraditional spelling of "Breakthru" solely in order to highlight our particular meaning for the Dream Maker Process. "Breakthru Dreaming" is meant to be a label for this process, and we feel the spelling change will help to keep the reader alerted to this fact.) The Dream Maker Process is a natural process which is opposed to the secondary process of censoring feelings. We have discovered the dynamics which make up the Dream Maker Process and we will teach you to become aware of them, identify them, and use them to change your dreams and feelings.

The fourth idea is that of the *Dream Maker Tradition.* As a person experiences Breakthru Dreams and Dream Maker Awareness he finds himself entering a new kind of community— a community which resembles some of the truest communities ever known. A new Dream Maker teaches people around him something they could never learn from books. A Dream Maker can spontaneously begin to help himself and others with dreams and feelings. Each new Dream Maker becomes a student and a teacher who can carry on the Dream Maker Tradition as a home-grown form of therapy and development, with no leaders and no followers.

We want the readers of this book to understand from the beginning that *making your dreams different means making your life different.* We have not written a simple weekend's entertainment to be read like a mystery story or western and then forgotten. Dreams can lead you far astray psychologically. Dabbling with your dreams and feelings can be very dangerous, but if you read and understand and begin to do what we did, your life will start to change for the better—and you will begin to enter the risky awareness of a Dream Maker.

There is another book which is related to *The Dream Makers* called *The Transformation of Dreams* which we have written with Lee Woldenberg, M.D., and Werner Karle, Ph.D. It is a technical book which reports, in full, our research, our theories, and our clinical observations. We mention it just to let you know that the ideas we present in popular form here have been extensively researched.

Our concern in *The Dream Makers* is not research and proof but "insearch" and experience. We want you to begin a search for your own Breakthru Dreams and Dream Maker. We invite you to experience all the excitement and adventure the search will bring.

It is important to let you know that the proving, refining, and explaining of our discoveries is still going on. We are not describing a new world which has been completely mapped, oc-cupied, or populated. The dream discoveries we have made are like large islands in a sea of unknowns. As yet, very few people know the way to these lands and even fewer live on them. Imagine yourself as a voyager. We are just voyagers who have preceded you; we are not architects who can give you finished plans for a new civilization.

Taking the analogy a little bit further, if you were shipwrecked and washed ashore on these strange, beautiful, and dangerous islands, who would you wish to meet first—a native or a visiting scientist? Our preference would be to first make friends with the native. The scientist might know the Latin names of plants and animals and be able to explain their evolutionary significance, but the native would know what was good to eat. In this book we will try to tell you which dreams you can eat and which ones might eat you. *The Dream Makers* is a survival manual and not a scientific treatise.

Nothing about dreams can be permanently learned by just reading; you need to *do* some things and notice what happens. At places in this book we will ask you to try some things which will help you to feel more about your life and to learn more about your dreams. Doing these exercises is as important as reading the book.

TRY THIS: Think about the last dream you can remember. Try to think about it as though you were telling the story of your dream to us. Add in the dialogue, the setting, the characters, and be sure to say how you felt at different times in the dream. Also be sure to say how you felt when you woke up from the dream. If you can remember no dreams whatsoever, think about a waking experience that had an impact on you; think about telling us the waking experience as if it were a dream. Now do nothing. We are the therapists. We will work with your dreams and your experiences throughout this book.

# Part One
# THE DREAM MAKER
# TRADITION

# 1
# The Breakthru Dream

❧ It was a time of crisis. People were calling for action, "Do something! Do something!" But Tarachiwa, the Iroquois shaman, was doing nothing. He was sitting alone under a lean-to of branches he had built deep in the forest. In the village other men were running about, making plans, changing plans, and arguing with one another.

Tarachiwa heard none of the arguments. He was asleep. What a strange way to meet a crisis! Still, Tarachiwa had met other crises in this way and he trusted his dreams. Four winters ago he had dreamt of how and where to organize an elk hunt and the tribe had survived the long severe winter from the success of Tarachiwa's hunt. Just last summer he had dreamt of a new way to make traps and now almost every hunter in the tribe was using the method he had learned in his dream.

But this crisis was different. Strange men had come to the tribe. They wore long black robes and talked of a new God called Jesus. They told the people to change from their old ways. White soldiers with guns came to protect the black robes.

Some people of the tribe wanted to kill all the black robes; others were attracted by the new Jesus God. Tarachiwa himself said little in the councils. He waited for the words to spring from deep within.

That night Tarachiwa did dream. In his dream the Dream Maker appeared as a black crow and said:

"Do not worry. The whites cannot persuade your people. Their words are not strong. But do not harm them or the guns of their soldiers will kill many of your people."

The next day Tarachiwa spoke at the council and told his dream to all the chiefs and to the people. After much talk they chose to follow Tarachiwa's dream. Thereafter the tribes did not harm the priests but neither did they become Christians. They continued to follow the old teachings and their own shamans.

Historical documents show us that even 125 years after the Jesuits had first visited the Iroquois they had been unable to convert them and unable to persuade the tribes to give up their dream practices. The spirit of the Dream Maker Tradition can be found in this Indian song:

> Sleep! Sleep!
> In the land of Dreams
> Find your Grown-Up Self
> Your future family
> Sleep! Sleep!

This Dream Maker Tradition has not been followed in modern times because most people today would find it very peculiar to think that they could find their "grown-up self" in the "land of dreams." Our modern society offers no widespread instruction in dreaming or in using dreams; there is certainly no special reliance upon dream guidance by groups.

Instead of following their inner teachers, people increasingly turn to outside teachers and adopt outside beliefs. Often when they are finished believing, they reflect and ask themselves why they are so disappointed. Most people eventually become disappointed in new methods and new leaders because they do not lead them to deep, heartfelt changes. When a person has Breakthru Dreams and gains his Dream Maker Awareness he must change from inside out.

## Rediscovering the Dream Maker Approach

Before we go on with the story of our own Breakthru Dreams we will summarize some of the basic ideas that eventually grew out of our discoveries. Of course, this is doing it backwards; the discoveries were made first and the labels and ideas came later. But this time, backwards is better because it will help you to clearly understand our story if you have in mind at least a rough map of how different and revolutionary the Breakthru Dreams really are.

We did not sit down one day and think up the Dream Maker Approach to dreams. What happened was that in 1971 a group of us (eight psychotherapists, one woman and seven men) established a new psychotherapy center where we could work together and try out a different way of practicing therapy. When we began we did not have a clear set of ideas about what to do or why we were doing things differently. We experimented on each other and then slowly passed on the experiences and insights to our patients.

Looking back, we can see that the main thing we did that was different from what other psychotherapists had done was that *we continued to be patients*. That was unusual; our entire staff of therapists continued to receive regular weekly therapy sessions from each other in which we would trade off the roles of patient and therapist. We also had regular weekly group sessions all together.

When we cut away all the theories and psychological mumbo jumbo we discovered that what really counted was not what someone was trying to do but who he or she was. It was a radical innovation that we continued to get more help and continued changing ourselves. We went beyond repair: we stopped believing in illness and we began to teach our patients about transforming their lives.

## The Breakthru Dream

Every now and then as we continued to help each other we would have dreams which were unlike any we had ever experienced or read about. These dreams did not require interpretation. They were not symbolic, coded messages from the unconscious which had to be deciphered.

Without knowing it we had found the second way to dream—the one that works; normal dreams do not work. The two kinds of dreams are: (1) *normal dreams* which require interpretation. They are usually passive and full of anxiety. They don't work. And (2) *Breakthru Dreams* which do not require interpretation. The dream involves the dreamer and teaches him directly about his life.

Slowly these new kinds of dreams began to teach us about dreams in general and about our lives. We began to learn that what everyone thought was the unconscious was simply a grab bag of unexpressed feelings from the day and from the past. We began to see that if we could be conscious enough during the day to express *all* of our feelings then we could have different kinds of dreams at night.

Eventually we began to call these new kinds of dreams Breakthru Dreams because they were a direct breakthrough between the unconscious and the conscious. In a Breakthru Dream the dreamer is aware and able to clearly express all feelings. Sounds simple—it isn't. It's basic but it is not easy.

Dream psychologists have collected and classified tens of thousands of "normal" dreams. What they conclude from these collections is that the normal dream is typically passive, apprehensive, and somewhat unpleasant. Usually the normal dreamer is not aware he is dreaming and he is not active or expressive in his dreams; often he is merely an observer. The feeling level in normal dreams is generally low and there is frequently a "gray area" between reality and fantasy.

The Breakthru Dream contrasts strongly with normal dreaming and gives a perspective on all other kinds of dreams. Here is a Breakthru Dream of one of our staff:

*I was parachuting down to a beautiful island in the South Pacific. As I slowly descended I knew that I was dreaming and I knew the natives on the island would worship me as a god; they had a mythology that predicted someone would come from the sky to lead them. Because of this I realized I could have almost anything I wanted from them. I also knew that they were an almost perfect culture. They were physically beautiful, loving, and free from violence and crime. I knew they needed only one more thing to make their life perfect and I would bring that to them. Then I was walking up to their village from the beach where I had landed. They were all running toward me and I could see how strong and beautiful they were. I saw them waving to me and I waved back at them. I noticed that I could feel good because they thought I was good and powerful. Then we gathered around a campfire in the village. I suddenly realized what I had that I could give them. It was the final knowledge they were waiting for and I had it. Just knowing what I was about to say affected me. I could clearly feel inside myself how I was giving up the false image they had of me. As I gave it up I felt more and more feelings of power and sadness inside of me. "There are no leaders," is what I told them. I suddenly felt much closer to them. I felt a sense of relief go through my body. I had friends in my life instead of being separate. I began to cry and told them how glad I was to be there. As I looked closer, I saw that they were actually my friends—Steve, Carole, Riggs, Joe, Dominic, Jerry, Werner—and they were all gathered around me.*

Notice that this dream has a number of characteristics which distinguish it from an ordinary dream. First, the dreamer is aware that he is dreaming. Second, the dream is full of feeling. Third, the dreamer fully expresses the feelings he has. And fourth, the dream shifts from a symbolic, unreal mode to a real representation of the dreamer's life with his friends.

These characteristics clearly identify Breakthru Dreams. *They are present any time the natural process of feeling is carried to the limit in dreaming.*

The four characteristics we have identified are the dynamics of the Dream Maker Process. (Later in the book we will teach you to work with and chart your dreams using these dynamic processes.)

The classic psychoanalytic theory holds that dreams are disguised wish fulfillments. Freud postulated the existence of a dream work mechanism or censor to convert blatant, socially unacceptable wishes (usually sexual wishes) into disguised symbolic pictures.

What we learned from our attempts to share all our feelings and dreams was that *the censoring process is a secondary process.* It is certainly true that people do learn to disguise and hold back their wishes and other feelings. But it is also true that *people have a primary impulse to express feelings completely and openly. In short, there is a basic thrust, in waking and dreaming, toward full consciousness. We call this the Dream Maker Process.*

When the Dream Maker Process prevails, then, symbolic, confused, and censored dreams are transformed into direct, clear, and expressive dreams—Breakthru Dreams. These new dreams provide a feeling reference for what waking and dreaming can be. Breakthru Dreams merge the realism and self-control of waking consciousness with the emotional energy of dream consciousness.

## The Dream Maker

At places in this book we will personify the Dream Maker Process and talk about "the Dream Maker." Of course we do not believe in a Dream Maker who exists inside our heads, like the sandman, to bring us dreams. Nor did Freud believe that there was a "Censor" who stood at the doorway to consciousness admitting or rejecting or disguising certain contents. Both the Dream Maker and the Censor are psychological processes and we will go into considerable detail throughout the book to explain how the Dream Maker Process works.

However, it is sometimes of real value to talk about the Dream Maker as though he was a person or a power. (For simplicity, from here on we will refer to the Dream Maker as "he.") The value of this mythic way of talking is that it matches the way we experience dreams, especially very intense dreams.

Everyone knows how foreign and outside his self-control nightmares seem to be. We often feel as though we've been invaded by an outside force or being. What has "invaded us" is actually what we already have inside of ourselves—the thrust toward reality which conflicts with our learned ways of avoiding real feelings. The Breakthru Dream represents the victory of the Dream Maker over the Censor, of the force for full and clear expression over the habits of repression.

After we had experienced Breakthru Dreams for several years we were able to begin to describe what was happening in dreams and begin to teach our patients how they could learn to use their dreams in a new way. We also began to extend the use of this Dream Maker Approach beyond the confines of psychotherapy.


We make a claim in this book that we have found a revolutionary method to make your dreams and feelings work for you. You are going to read about how a group of people changed, how they changed the people around them, and how you can change, too.

In the Dream Maker Tradition there is nothing to believe— there is only the knowing that comes from new experiences. As you read this book you will be initiated into a new awareness— the Dream Maker Awareness. The first step toward that awareness is to recognize whether your dreams are working for you or against you.

Most people's dreams and feelings work against them. This means that they go to bed with a minus and they wake up in the morning with a minus. When a person has a dream that works for him, he wakes up with a plus; he feels good, he has no debts to pay back. And as he lives from this plus starting point he has a day full of feelings. We are starting a mental health revolution that can be understood if you know the difference between plus and minus.

Breakthru Dreaming is a natural, effective way to dream but it can appear strange and threatening. A peculiar thing happens to most people as they grow up: they stop dreaming naturally and learn to dream normally, in a mixed-up and unreal way just like everyone else. After a while, people come to believe that "dreams just are symbolic and confusing." They do not have to be.

What we want to do in this book is teach you how to change your dreams and feelings so that they begin working for you. Then you can find what our earliest ancestors knew—Dream Maker Awareness.

# Part Two
## DISCOVERING THE DREAM MAKER

# 2
# The Dream Maker
# Visits

Let us begin by telling you how we came to understand and feel and use our dreams differently. It did not happen to us all at once, but if we had to pick a certain time it would have been in the summer of 1973 . . . when we first began to experience recognizable Breakthru Dreams.

You will first meet Dominic, a psychologist and colleague at the Center for Feeling Therapy. You will learn how Dominic changed as he met the Dream Maker. In the story you will also meet Lee, Werner, Jerry, Steve, and Carole, our other friends. When we talk about Riggs and Joe we are talking about ourselves (R. C. and J. H.). All of us, together, rediscovered the Dream Maker Tradition and each of us met the Dream Maker.

We will be presenting our own brief "case" histories and a few of those of our colleagues in order to illuminate in a personal and, hopefully, meaningful way the nature of the Dream Maker Process. We are not detached professionals; rather we are involved in our work personally . . . the Dream Maker has changed our lives. By reading about our change, and then seeing the Process which has developed in Parts Three and Four, we hope the Breakthru Dream has a fertile and clear meaning for you. A dry analysis of the Process would be lacking for most readers, as would a series of anecdotes with no explanation. Taken together though, the Dream Maker Tradition should hold greater meaning and effectiveness for you.

## Dominic—The First Breakthru

*The city is Los Angeles. It is late. Only the night people are out on the streets: hookers and worn-out businessmen, policemen and winos. In the houses, many people have left their lights on and locked their dead bolt locks to keep away late-night intruders. But this night there is another kind of intruder in Los Angeles— someone that locks won't keep out, someone the police cannot chase. And that intruder is coming to one man, as he sleeps.*

*The man is Dominic. He is no longer young—but not quite middle-aged. He is slowing down a little. All the false promises of his youth are fading. He has made it to where he should be in his profession. He is a partner in a successful clinic. He is a good psychotherapist. But all that Dominic is aware of this night are bad dreams—and poor sleep. Something is happening to him and he doesn't know what.*

In many ways Dominic would have been better off to have met another kind of intruder. He would have forgotten about him in time or collected on his insurance for stolen goods. But there will be no forgetting or insurance, because Dominic is about to experience an event that will change his life. He is about to have a certain kind of dream—a Breakthru Dream— which is so different from other dreams and other waking experiences that it will shake him for the rest of his life.

In short, Dominic's coming dream experiences could be seen as a breakthrough or snapping within his mind. What is going to happen is that the barriers between his unconscious mind, in which his feelings, power, and creativity are stored, and his conscious mind, which he uses to control his life, are going to break. When they do, there will be a snap, a breakthrough, and all the power and energy of the unconscious will be freed and blended with the control and decision-making of his conscious mind.

*As Dominic lay in his bed, all he could feel was a tightness in his throat. The more aware he became of it, the more afraid he became. He was dreaming. But he was awake—or was he? He didn't know. Dreaming or awake. Small beads of sweat built up along his neck and forehead. The fear filled the air around him. Each breath brought him more fear and tightness.*

*Something had startled him. He stared across the dark room. He could just make out someone's figure. The hair along his arms and neck was prickling. There was a man or someone standing in his room. Dominic looked intently with his dreaming eyes. His body was rigid with fear. He told himself that he was dreaming. He tried to move, he couldn't. He tried to close his eyes, he couldn't.*

*The figure moved. The man was beckoning him, motioning Dom to come closer. Dominic thought he was going to be killed. He could feel his heart pounding. This strange and ominous figure motioned or moved. Dom wished someone else was sleeping in the house.*

What Dominic was going through had happened to others before him, but they had forgotten it, or tried to forget it; they lived within a tradition of forgetfulness. The Iroquois did not try to forget; they learned to use Breakthrus and make them work. But at the time Dominic did not know there was a tradition that could have helped him, that many people before him had learned the connection between the night and the day.

*Dominic fought the paralysis of sleep. He forced himself to shout. "Get out! Get out of here!" As he shouted the dream faded. He was safe. He realized it was just a dream. What he did not realize was that this dream was a beginning.*

Dominic was beginning; his first night was like a hint. What Dominic did not know was that he was about to experience three days and nights in which he would be dragged into the world of the Dream Maker, unable to escape from it.

The dream experience that happened the first night was not a Breakthru Dream; those would come later and Dominic would need help in finding his Breakthru Dream. It would be painful for him.

*Dominic had chased the dream away. As he woke up he was sitting in a tangled mess of sheets and blankets and pillows. He turned on the light. It was four-thirty. His eyes got heavy as his tired body invited him to more sleep. There would be no more bad dreams tonight.*

As the clock rang, signaling that it was time to get going, Dominic rolled out of bed and began to get ready for work. He needed to be in good shape. He was a therapist, a very good therapist, probably one of the very best. As Dominic shaved and dressed he thought about the coming day's work. The dream would come back to him in little flashes. The coffee was boiling and Dominic was trying to forget. He did not remember all the other times the Dream Maker had come to him. This man, this figure in his dreams, had haunted him for years. They had never met but now that was about to change. Dominic was getting closer to his first meeting with the Dream Maker.

After drinking his coffee Dominic thought about getting some help. He lives next door to Riggs but he couldn't bring himself to walk over and talk. Instead, he drove to work alone, thinking about his dreams and about asking Riggs for help. As he drove and remembered last night he felt a little scared. Dominic got to work and almost asked Riggs for help—but he didn't. His voice felt stuck in his throat.

The Dream Maker watched Dominic. Like a savage Zen master, he would not relent in his pursuit of Dominic. Dominic was close, all the years of giving in to his feelings and getting help from his friends had prepared him for the Dream Maker;

he needed only to take a few more steps and it would happen. But those steps—those words—Dominic was having trouble letting them out. He was tired from the bad night's sleep.

All the other therapists had already started before Dominic went into his room to begin working with his patient. He worked for a little over two hours. It had been a very good session; the young woman he was seeing was really letting go and expressing intense feelings. By the time he finished most of the other therapists were gone. Dominic looked for Riggs. "I know he's the one—he can help me." Silently Dominic asked, "Riggs, help me." He heard Riggs's four-wheel drive start up. It sounded like a race car.

Riggs sat silently in his car. "Something is wrong," he thought. He knew it—he could sense it but he didn't know what. As he backed the car out he saw Dominic walking out of the building. He drove home.

Dominic wanted to run after him but he didn't. He wanted to ask for help with something he feared but he was also afraid to ask. Maybe he would get more help than he wanted. As Dominic drove home his attention kept lapsing. It was becoming difficult to drive; the Dream Maker was not waiting for sleep. Dominic, feeling sick and sleepy, shook himself and drove into town. He had two meetings: one with the Center's lawyer, the other with the accountant.

He finally got home about six-thirty but sat in his car for a while. In all of his life he had never felt so bad. He needed help right now. He felt paralyzed as a few tears rolled down his face.

Riggs's home office looks out onto the street. He saw Dominic drive up and the foreboding feeling returned. He watched Dominic sit there. Dominic was wondering what to do when he heard Riggs's voice, "Are you okay, Dom?"

"Riggs, help me. I don't know what's wrong. Something terrible is happening to me."

Riggs didn't wait. He got into Dominic's car and drove to the Center, arriving around seven o'clock. Riggs led Dominic into one of the soundproof therapy rooms and told him to lie down.

Dominic stared up at the dim light. He could not tell whether he was dreaming or awake. Dominic was in a halfway place between awareness and unconsciousness; he must either wake up to his feelings or drift into a dimmer awareness. Riggs knew from his years of experience as a therapist that what was needed was some direction of movement—something to bring Dominic's awareness into action. But the direction was not yet clear, all he could do was keep reminding Dom that he was not alone.

Every now and then Riggs's voice would intrude into Dom's halfway world. As Riggs's voice broke the trance it seemed penetrating—something Dominic wanted to get away from.

Dominic was uneasy. Time had somehow slowed down, working against him. He wanted the therapy session to be over, but this session wouldn't end in time. "God, I know it won't end soon enough." Dominic felt sick to his stomach.

Riggs sat and watched him, then he stood up and began walking around the large consulting room. Riggs had known Dominic for over ten years but at this moment it was as if they had never met; Dominic felt like a stranger. Dom could hardly remember what had prompted him to ask for help, to become a patient once again. Those thoughts drifted away and he came back to reality. He was lying on the floor talking about a dream. Dominic stared at Riggs, tall and powerful. As he walked around Dominic watched him.

"What was the dream trying to show you, Dominic?"

"Nothing, I don't know." Dominic felt confused, the more questions he was asked the more his mind went blank.

Riggs waited for answers in the semilit room. He could see Dominic squirm and twist away from what his dream was bringing him, but he knew he must wait. As he waited Riggs remembered his own dream.

*I was looking out across the room. I thought I was awake. I saw figures of many people, all of them in pain—terrible and tortuous pain. I asked out loud, "What do you want me to do?" I got no answer. I began to cry. The pain I witnessed seemed to break my heart. I felt no end to my crying.*

He remembered the old dream and changes it had brought him and ever since, had always seen people differently; he was not quite so hard on them or himself. Riggs did not know it then but that dream was more than a dream. It was something special—the beginning of his Breakthru.

At first Riggs didn't know what exactly to do with Dominic. He had two guideposts—his own dream and his feelings for Dom. They were good, close friends.

Dominic felt frantic. Time wouldn't pass. "How long does a session last?" Today it seemed like forever. Riggs would not relent. Dominic saw him looking at his watch and wondered if he was finally getting tired, maybe tired enough to leave and end it.

"Dominic, we aren't going to leave. I want you to find that dream again so that you can feel what's underneath all those scary pictures."

Dominic tried to remember the dream. He tried to think. There was something he couldn't remember.

Riggs had indications for several weeks that something was going on with Dom—vague, discreet warnings. Dom was, like everyone on the staff at our clinic, *really trying*. "Really trying." In waking, it sounds so good, a good topic for discussion, but at night—in the world of sleep and dreams—"trying" can be swallowed up without so much as a whimper.

Sometimes Dominic would be "out of it" for a while, not quite right—but those things are normal. "Normal," another nice word in waking. But in the darkness of a bedroom, in the midst of sleep, normal doesn't count for much.

Now Riggs regretted not interfering sooner. They had begun the session at seven in the evening; it was now ten-thirty. Riggs said, "Dom, if you can't remember how you felt in that dream I'm going to stay right here with you until you have another."

Then Riggs went out to the staff room and got himself a cup of coffee. When he returned he brought a blanket and a pillow and said, "Make yourself comfortable, we're staying."

It was twelve-thirty before Dominic uneasily went to sleep. Riggs sat in the corner and read through some research articles under a dim light.

The Dream Maker rarely comes to a person openly; instead he mixes with dream fragments or daytime thoughts which do not pass. Dominic had been having those kinds of thoughts and dreams for years. In some ways his mind was full of signs, or direction markers, left as if by instinct for the Dream Maker to follow.


Dominic was at last having a pleasant dream. He felt safer with Riggs in the room. The Dream Maker followed that dream. In fact, he had made that dream because he knew Dominic would not stop it. Dominic would enjoy this dream, letting himself go a little further than usual and drifting closer to the uncensored region of the Dream Maker.

*I was dreaming that I was walking down the street. I felt as if I was seeing things for the first time. The trees were bright green. The sun was shining. The more I walked the better I felt. My body felt alive and full of pleasure. Then everything became brighter and brighter. I walked and began seeing things I had never seen before.*

As Dominic drifted amid the dream pleasure, he sensed something was wrong. The dream was changing. His body sensations were too strong; he couldn't control them. As the dream changed, the Dream Maker made himself known.

*I tried to cover my eyes. Things were too bright. Something was happening beyond the brightness. I couldn't see what it was. I tried to turn around. I couldn't move. I had gone too far. I felt as if I was on the edge of some tremendous realization. I didn't want to know what it was. I felt terrified—like something had a hold on me and was taking me someplace. I didn't want to go. I felt as if I was losing my mind. Something was drawing me closer.*

Riggs was a trained scientist. He watched Dominic as he slept and noticed Dom's breathing suddenly changing and becoming more rapid. Riggs knew Dominic was dreaming. Abruptly, Dom sat up. He looked startled; there was a light perspiration on his face and neck.

"What is it?" Riggs asked.

"I don't know—a dream, a real scary dream."

"Keep talking, Dom."

"Riggs, I feel very scared—like I'm standing on the edge. I'm afraid to look over, but worse than that—I feel like someone's trying to push me over. I just want to get rid of it, forget it."

Like the millions of other people who slept and dreamt that night, Dominic would try to forget. But Riggs would not let him. The Dream Maker and Riggs had finally taken him deep enough—deeper than forgetting. Riggs told him, "You're going to stay on the edge until you go over and that's going to be soon. Let's go home for now."

As he crawled out of bed the next morning, Dominic was unhappy, confused, and disappointed. He had been through two long nights in a row. As he washed himself, he looked into the mirror and talked out loud. He was a therapist and he knew how to help himself, but the help he was giving out didn't seem to work this morning. By the time he finished his second cup of coffee he wondered if he hadn't been too hasty in giving up cigarettes.

He left for work with the feeling that something was wrong.

He thought to himself that he might have had too much therapy, maybe gotten in over his head. Dominic was no hero, but he felt like there was a war going on inside his head. He pulled himself together, had another cup of coffee at the office, and then went in to see his patient.

What we would eventually come to understand is that dreams are secondary; the Dream Maker comes first because he creates dreams out of what is hidden in each person to force their awakening. A person who comes awake becomes a Dream Maker. Dominic's dreams were only a part of what he would have to experience to become a Dream Maker.

His second dream was a dream within a dream; it was not a normal dream. That dream was more of a statement about his life, conveying direct feelings about what was happening inside of him.

The Dream Maker is direct, bluntly truthful. There is no "Yes, please" or "I don't think so" in the Dream Maker's world. There are bumps, punches in the stomach that say, "Wake up! There is something more to you than your silly waking and sleeping fantasies." The Dream Maker is not civilized. He is life and death—nothing less. Dominic was entering the time of becoming a Dream Maker—a time of terror and intensity.

The next night Riggs sat up reading and thinking. He had all of his books about Indian tribes and different groups of ancient dreamers spread out on his desk. From what he could understand they somehow seemed the closest to what was happening to Dominic. It was as if Dominic was beginning to experience what the Indians and other primitive people had found as a way of helping themselves. "God, I guess I'll have to go it on instinct," thought Riggs.

Riggs was worried about Dom. He didn't know exactly what to do except to keep Dominic from forgetting. It seemed critical to remind him to pay attention to his dreams.

By the time Dominic got into bed, he wasn't listening to Riggs or anyone. He turned on the TV and watched aimlessly, waiting for sleep.

Everybody wants something special, but few want to go through what they must to attain it. Dominic didn't want to; he had begun to fight the most powerful force in his body, and he fought by trying not to pay attention to how he was feeling. As he fought, he was being ushered into another domain. Dominic's fighting could not hold back the Dream Maker. The Dream Maker waited; the new dreams he had created would not stay covered over.

As Dominic settled in for the night and tried to get to sleep, the Dream Maker was there. Dom couldn't get comfortable; he thought he must have eaten too much. He felt hot and nauseous, but couldn't vomit. He went back to bed and switched channels on the TV. As usual there was nothing. A few talk shows talking about talking. "What dull shit," he thought.

He didn't admit then that many things *he* did were dull—of course, professionally dull. He let himself say and do things that didn't feel quite right. To everyone else he was okay. Very okay. No one trembled when he came into a room. He was good, better than most, but not the best Dominic, definitely not the best *for* Dominic. He was more, he knew it, but he let that slide the same way he let his dreams go.

By 12:45 A.M. Dominic shut off the TV; he was tired and drifted into sleep. His body sank, allowing the sleep mechanism to take over, ready to give up control, to let sleep give him a reprieve. He did not know the Dream Maker was waiting. This night the Dream Maker first appeared in disjointed dream fragments mixed with other dreams. He had been asleep for four and a half hours before the Dream Maker worked his way through the day's defenses. Now, asleep and deeply relaxed, Dom was no longer confused.

The Dream Maker created a dream. The same dream as the night before, but this time the Dream Maker took him further into a new dream world and did more damage to his "normality."

*I was walking down the street. Everything was beautiful. I started looking at trees. The greens of the leaves were intense. And then I realized that this dream was the same one that I had the night before. I turned to run. The way back was becoming brighter and brighter. In every direction I looked there was a wonderful and terrifying brightness. I knew I had to get out of there. I could feel my head pounding. I felt as if I was being changed. I didn't want it. I was afraid I was being changed into someone who wasn't really me. I started to run. The more I ran the more I realized that something was chasing me, someone or something that I was afraid of. Something that could do something to me.*

Alone and in the middle of the night Dominic did what anyone of us would do—fight! He fought the paralysis and lack of control that sleep brings. He fought to make the dream "just a dream," to put all the perceptions and feelings of the dream outside himself and label them a nightmare. He did not want to know what he knew or to meet the Dream Maker.

As Dominic began to wake up he tried to make sense out of what was happening to him. He felt disoriented and stumbled for the light; he couldn't seem to get fully awake. He finally got up and went into his kitchen, to make some tea. As he put on the kettle he asked himself, "What's wrong with me? What haven't I said or done?" Back and forth he went. His image of who he was tried to weave a spell around the dream. The Dream Maker would wait, just as he had waited for hundreds of years, for millions of people. He had done his job that night. Dominic was awake and would not be getting back to sleep; the Dream Maker had won the night.

The middle of the night is a good time for a person to think about his life—what it means, how it's being lived. Dominic did just that. He pondered and returned again and again to the dream as he might scratch an itchy sore; he was bringing the dream into waking. Without knowing it, he had begun to think as a Dream Maker.

Everybody believes there is something special in them, something hidden deep inside. Sometimes people act especially bad, especially good, especially good-looking, especially smart. Those are only pictures. The Dream Maker destroys pictures. He brings people close to the realization of what is really inside.

Dominic drank his tea and honey slowly; he had lots of time. Morning and the hustle and bustle of working seemed very distant. He sat in his kitchen and remembered his dreams. For three nights in a row they or it had come and he still could not figure anything out.

Around 5:00 A.M. he took a short walk. The hustle of the city was still more than an hour away. For the first time in a long while Dominic felt different. He wasn't in a hurry. The grayness crept into the sky as everything around him was becoming brighter. He felt safe in the coming day, more removed from the night.

Dominic walked for over an hour and a half. He carried his empty tea cup with him. By the time Dominic got to the clinic his face was a little tired and strained. He drank no coffee. He thought maybe, just maybe, the coffee was disturbing his sleep.

All day long he was bothered by the dream feelings. Anything said to him seemed too loud or too harsh. The world he saw was drab. He couldn't shake the dream, even in waking. The Dream Maker was close throughout the day.

Dominic felt numb. Anyone can recognize people who have missed their awakenings because they look numbed, defeated, old before their time. Oh, they can talk and laugh, do things, "carry on," but something is missing. They know it, but they don't know where they missed it.

The first adult encounters with the Dream Maker are like nightmares, but worse. They fill the dreamer with body sensations. They make him feel his dream—the condition of his life. If the dream is faced, felt, and lived, it changes; it becomes gentler, a source of deep pleasure and insight.

But Dominic was not there now; he was in the first stages. The ferocity of the fight was debilitating. He was fighting for what he thought was his sanity, but what was in fact insanity—a reasonable insanity that would keep him the same way until he died. The crisis was evident in retrospect. Either he would "let go" and allow the dream to change him, or he would find a stalemate, an endpoint, a lifelong cul-de-sac.

Dominic got home that afternoon about four, played a little basketball, felt awkward and uncoordinated. He talked bitterly to himself, called himself a spastic. Later he took a long hot bath and got ready for a dinner date with his girl friend Linda. All through dinner he was preoccupied, moody. He talked to Linda but wound up fighting over some ridiculous point. Like a well-scripted play or plot, Dom would be alone.

When he got home he went over to see Riggs. "I don't feel very good, Riggs."

"I don't believe you, Dom. I think you feel different and you don't know what to do with it. Let your feelings change you. I think you are close to some important stuff, I don't know what, but I have a hunch we'll find out soon enough."

Dominic thought about what Riggs, his trusted colleague, had said. "Don't worry, Dominic. I'll be here to help you. Something good is beginning to happen."

More than anything, he knew he was tired. He got into bed right away but was soon up again and put on four of his favorite record albums. He knew this would do it. "Sleep—heavenly sleep."

As Dominic slept, the Dream Maker came. Dominic had gone too far in his life searching for that something special. And now he would realize he had entered the world of the Dream Maker, a world from which he would never return. He was once again in that brightness.

*I looked around me—there was nothing familiar, except this painful brightness. I felt ecstatic and terrified. It was so bright I couldn't see. My eyes hurt so much they began to water. Tears started to roll down my face. I felt as if I was in a world of sadness. My eyes were closed and I began to see me. Lots of different me's. I saw all the roles and games I played. I cried more and more. I felt as if I had finally gotten to what I had wanted all of my life. I felt at home inside of myself. I was crying uncontrollably. I knew I would never be the same. I knew what I had been running from all of my life–me. The more I cried, the happier I became. I was crying and laughing. I was laughing louder and louder. The louder I laughed, the more I could feel my chest expand. Everything seemed familiar. My friends were all standing around. I opened my arms to them shouting, "Reality. I have found Reality. Reality, welcome to Reality."*

At last Dominic had experienced a full Breakthru Dream. His awareness had been so altered at night that he would not be able to settle for anything less when awake. We did not know it then, but he was also going to draw us all into the Dream Maker Tradition.

TEST YOURSELF. In Part Three we will teach you day by day how to have your own Breakthru Dreams. For now begin to prepare yourself by comparing your life situation to Dominic's. Ask yourself the following questions; if you can answer yes to three of the five questions you are ready to experience Breakthru Dreams:
1) Do you *talk* about how you feel with your friends?
2) Are you able to *show* how you feel with your friends?
3) Do you sometimes take advice from your friends?
4) Do you give advice to your friends?
5) Do you talk about your dreams with friends?

The awakening Dominic was now first experiencing—the Breakthru Dream and the Dream Maker Awareness—was familiar to other people in other times. For instance, the Senoi, a tribe in Malaysia, had found something similar to it at least 350 years earlier. They practiced the Dream Maker Tradition, lost it, and regained it.

For years they were known as "the dream people," and were feared even by the most savage tribesmen who lived in their territory because of the Senoi's "specialness," their power. They were nonviolent; there was no mental illness in their society, no crime.

They cultivated the world of the dream. In their dreams they faced the fears they knew from the day. For them dreams had become naturally curative; their dream world healed the pains of growing up and the fears of jungle tigers.

Then their country and their dream world was torn by the second world war. Different armies fought to win over these jungle-wise people as soldiers and guides. The Senoi did not believe all their words. It was the guns and watches and jewelry that caught their eyes. As they began to change, their dream world no longer taught them. They were once fearless warriors in their dreams and now they were becoming scared children. They had once learned to be awake in their dreams and talk to tears and happiness, but now they dreamt only colorless, confusing stories. They were no longer "the dream people."

*Not everyone lost the Dream Maker Tradition. Baleh was a halak, a leader, a tohat, a knower of dreams. Baleh would not listen to the ticking of the watches. He saw his people losing their way of life.*

*It was near the end of the first summer of the war. Baleh wanted to return his people to the way of dreams. He sought a dream to teach him. At last the dream came to him and told him of a place deep in the jungle, a place far away from the war and the lies. He had found the answer.*

*But his people would not listen. Baleh was despondent. His head told him it was no use. He should go away with the English, too. But his heart talked only of the Great Dream of saving his people. He slept throughout the afternoon. The dream returned but this time the Dream Maker showed him a new dance to give his people: the dance of war and the dance of the Senoi. Baleh did not waken until the evening drums had begun to beat. He got up and approached his people. He began to sing of his dream and to dance. As he danced he wept. He told the story of how his people and their way of life was dying. The people began to hear him. Slowly they began joining him. Each new dancer allowed himself to weep the tears of the Great Dream.*

*Not everyone heard or wanted to hear the dream. Many did. Baleh led the listeners off into the deepest jungle. There was no place special—there was the specialness of going. Baleh and his people regained their dream life. They were once again the dream people. Once again the Dream Maker Tradition endured through the dreams of a single dreamer.*

# 3
# The Dream Maker Stays

For the first time in four days Dominic woke up feeling great. He called Linda the very first thing and asked her to come over. They excitedly talked over breakfast, glad to be close again.

Dominic drove to work early, feeling ten years younger. In the clinic staff room he threw open his arms and shouted, "Reality. Welcome to Reality." Everyone began shouting and joking back and forth, "Reality, welcome to Reality." It was like a song. We were all laughing and talking. Dominic told us what he had been through the past four nights. The more he talked, the quieter we all became.

Riggs had helped the dream become a reality. Their last therapy session had been long and painful, much like a difficult childbirth, but now the child was free. Riggs sat and watched Dominic enjoy his newfound freedom.

What Riggs and Dominic and Tarachiwa and Baleh had in common were their dreams. When a dream has waking consequences it means that the feelings in the dream no longer stay hidden behind symbolic pictures; the dream feeling pushes forward to be lived out in waking. But for each one of these special people there was a catch, a responsibility.

Riggs had lived out of his dream. He had taken Dominic through the difficult days of an experience that changed Dominic's life, just like dream people have been doing for centuries. But now the dream tradition must be passed on. Dominic must live from his dream. He must teach someone else to find his own Dream Maker Awareness.

Dominic had learned that dreams are feelings. He did not interpret his dream; he lived it, dreaming a new kind of dream.

The discovery that we made, or remade, is that there is a way of dreaming which requires no interpretation. Freud and Jung covered the interpretation side of dreaming very well, but they never went further because their personal feelings remained tangled up in their theories.

## Freud and Jung

*The place is Vienna. It is early October. Two of the world's foremost therapists, Sigmund Freud and Carl Jung, have begun to develop a friendship, that, if it lasts, will change psychotherapy and influence medical psychology. As they sit and drink the thick aromatic coffee in the cafe, there is a sense of history about them.*

These men are struggling to change psychotherapy, but more importantly they are seeking something from each other. They want "something to happen" between them. Unknowingly, they are moving closer to a point—a crisis. Months pass and they travel to America. They are beginning to get the recognition they have long deserved.

*As they are traveling back from a successful turning point in the acceptance of their theories something happens.*

*Freud is asleep. He begins to dream and he is deeply troubled by what he has dreamt. He usually works with his dreams by interpreting them himself, a practice of self-analysis he will later reject for his followers. This dream is so troubling that after breakfast he spends time by himself trying to lessen its impact on him. Jung watches his mentor from a distance. He has the "impulse" to say something—to break out of his role as the lesser partner. Jung paces the deck. He tries to understand himself. He knows he is not being truthful to himself. Finally, after a day of torment, he decides what he must do.*

*After dinner Freud and Jung smoke and drink their coffee. Jung breaks the superficial talk, "Sigmund, today you seemed so very troubled."*

*"I am, Carl. I had a dream that I cannot seem to work through. There are parts of the interpretation that are incomplete."*

*As Jung later recalled it, this incident was a crisis point that was never met head-on. " . . . I found our relationship exceedingly valuable. I regarded Freud as an older, more mature and experienced personality, and felt like a son in that respect. But then something happened which proved to be a severe blow to the whole relationship.*

*"Freud had a dream—I would not think it right to air the problem it involved. I interpreted it as best I could, but added that a great deal more could be said about it if he would supply me with additional details from his private life. Freud's response to these words was a curious look. . . . Then he said, 'But I cannot risk my authority.' At that moment he lost it altogether . . . the end of our relationship was already foreshadowed. Freud was placing personal authority above truth."*


Just before the moment when Jung backed off and did not press and Freud retreated into himself, the Dream Maker was ready to emerge. The Dream Maker Tradition was potentially there, ready to be rediscovered between these two great men. Instead it would have to wait for other men in other places. Both Freud and Jung bypassed the earliest Dream Maker teaching. They did not act on their primary impulse to sense and express their dream feelings completely; instead, they continued to rely on the Dream Censor instead of the Dream Maker. Unfortunately, they would never find their way back to that time and place in which they could have entered the Dream Maker Tradition.

If they could have let go then, they would have gathered together all the great therapists—just as the Indian tribes gathered the great chiefs. They would have taught each other and relearned the Dream Maker Tradition.

Imagine what it would have been like if Sigmund Freud, Carl Jung, Alfred Adler, Sandor Ferenzi, Medard Boss, and other prominent therapists had lived together, shared dreams together, and continued to do therapy on each other. At the beginning of the week Freud would have helped Jung and at the end of the week Jung would have been Freud's therapist. They would have created a joint therapy with a community of founders. Instead they became the solitary founders of individual therapies.

These therapies have an unwritten rule which says a doctor must remain a doctor, and patients must remain patients. We do not believe in this rule. We believe that doctors, like fine instruments in a wonderful orchestra, must be continually retuned. There is nothing wrong with retuning. In fact it is critically important—otherwise the doctor begins to believe that because he knows about taking care of people he does not need to be helped himself.

Riggs and Dominic began to enjoy this same kind of relationship. Riggs had worked with Dominic and Dominic had dreamt his Breakthru Dream. Now Riggs hoped that Dominic would be able to help our therapists in a new way.

The Breakthru Dream does not take the dreamer to a place but to a shift in awareness—the dreamer awakens. Each night as he remembers his dreams he is reminded once again to make a further shift inside himself. Dominic did not know all of these things. All he knew was that he could see and sense things and people differently.

Of all the people around him, he saw Werner the clearest. He took all of his newfound energy and concentrated it on Werner. Dominic did not know it but he was trying to do what the Dream Maker Tradition requires: "Pass it along." Before a person can take many new steps he must fully learn the first steps by teaching them to someone else.

# Werner the Wunderkind

As a child Werner was a skinny kid; his thin shoulders looked like a coat hanger had been stuck inside his skin, while his little-boy ribs made him look frail. His slender legs revolted against being skinny and little: they were strong and muscular. It was these legs that became Werner's favorite pastime—running. Growing up in Germany, he had run in the countryside, and when his uncle brought the seven-year-old Werner, his brother, and his mother to America his legs became a way of keeping him from getting hurt.

They moved to east Los Angeles. It was a tough place to grow up in, maybe even a little tougher on a skinny kid who has a German accent. Other kids beat him up, but he ran, and each day he seemed to get faster and faster, until they were no longer catching him. But not being caught was not good enough.

A boy has pride and so it became harder and harder for Werner to run home scared and afraid. Soon he was running to secret places, places where he could rest and let no one else know that he had run.

Very few people knew that as an adult Werner kept running from scary people and situations. Instead of using his legs he would run in his head. He forced his legs to keep him standing still, but inside he was running from what he *thought* people would think and say about him.

But the running in Werner's head was not taking him fast enough or far enough. Dominic kept pace with him, telling him there was more than research and hard work. To Werner, Dominic was just another person to be outrun. It used to be so easy to run to those remote places where no one could follow. But now Dominic followed, closely.

It was easy for Dominic to follow because Werner wanted help from Dominic—but only a certain kind of help. He wanted Dominic to keep him repaired so that he could work hard and feel good. But Dominic was not satisfied with that; he knew there was more to Werner than just hard work.

"You're going to have to slow down, Werner. The Nobel Prize will wait," Dominic told him.

Werner did not like waiting—he was not used to it. He had trouble getting enough rest. He thought that he needed to push through it. The Dream Maker was affecting Werner. His insides were no longer right.

Something was happening to Werner, but no one could pinpoint it. There was a general uneasiness among the staff. Riggs and Dominic spent a lot more time together, and each night Riggs would sit and read, searching for some explanation of whatever it was.

The uneasiness began to grow as we all sensed something brewing. Werner was starting to fight more and more with Dominic.

It had been over two months since the first Breakthru Dream occurred, but another was coming. Werner was beginning to break under the steady pressure Dom was applying to him. "You know, Dom, you keep telling me to slow down with this, to rethink that—how the hell do you think the research will get done?"

"It's not the research, Werner. It's you—the way you talk and act—you're always running scared behind that cool front."

Werner stared at Dominic. He felt as if he were looking the wrong way through a pair of binoculars and Dom was far away. The Dream Maker was breaking through. The wall between Werner's conscious and unconscious was crumbling. Werner struggled to snap out of it. He remembered a childhood nightmare.

*School is over and I start to walk home. I see these tough kids in front of me. Some of them are the same kids who have beaten me up before. I am really scared. I start to run. I am running as fast as I can. They're chasing me. They're right behind me. I keep running. I am out of breath.*

That was how he felt—running scared. The Dream Maker's voice became louder in Werner's head. He could hear Dominic talking, but still he felt far away.

"Werner, goddamit—say something and stop spacing out."

"What do you want me to say?" Werner tried to cover up what was happening.

Dom got tired of pushing him and finally relented. "Fuck it, Werner, but just remember, I'll get to you. You'll need me and then you'll know what I'm telling you."

Werner thought to himself, "Don't fucking threaten me, I'll never break."

In one way Werner was right. Dominic would not break him—the Dream Maker would. The Dream Maker listened and waited. He knew Werner was upset. He had listened in on everything that was said and thought.

Werner worked harder than ever that night. It was well past 3:00 A.M. before he finally stopped. He was keyed up and needed to drink two full glasses of wine before his cortex shut down. He didn't fall asleep, he crashed. There was no middle ground for Werner—only up or down. As he slept and dreamt he wished he had a middle ground or a friend. Dominic had been right.

*I am in a large hotel. My room is high over the city. I am enjoying the view when the fire alarm starts ringing. I run outside and the hall is filled with smoke. I run toward the exit. I begin running down the stairs. I keep running. I get more and more tired. There is much smoke.*

*I am choking and running. I lose my sense of direction. I can hardly tell whether I am running away from the fire or into it. The stairs almost seem flattened out. I don't know the way out any longer. I woke up exhausted and depressed.*

Werner got up around 8:30 A.M. It was Sunday and he was going to the motorcycle races. He had a bad taste in his mouth, and his brain felt fried. The dream had left him with a scared feeling. He tried to shake it off as he loaded his Yamaha into the trailer. He had a feeling that he wouldn't do well today; he felt too edgy, too scared.

The weather in Los Angeles late that summer was almost tropical. The days were hot and muggy and when it is hot for so long, the ending of summer is like the ending of winter in most places. Werner could sense that the weather was changing.

He got home late in the afternoon and went out to dinner with his girl friend, Laurie. He thought about the talk he and Dominic had on Friday. "I wonder what he means, that I have to stop running," he thought.

What Dominic told Werner did and did not make sense. He wanted to stop running but the thought of it seemed like too much. And he didn't know how he could possibly stop running—especially when "something was happening."

By the time dessert had been served, Werner was feeling pretty good. He and his girl friend walked along Sunset Boulevard and looked into the boutiques. Werner had a satisfied feeling and was able to put all his troublesome thoughts out of his mind. "It's been a really good day." That statement was a little premature.

The brass bed and the redwood walls were comfortable, secure. Werner took a long bath and visited with Laurie. They were beginning to know each other. By twelve-thirty Werner was exhausted. He turned off the light and curled next to her soft body. As he began his descent into the world of sleep, someone entered the room and waited. The more relaxed Werner became the closer this familiar stranger came. Like a maestro, this someone who Werner had never seen but often felt, began to direct Werner's dreams:

*We were all sitting around a large banquet room in a Holiday Inn laughing, talking, and eating when suddenly, someone outside was yelling that the building was on fire. Within seconds flames were all around us and we were all running out the door to get outside.*

Werner ran in his dream, but something was wrong—something was very different. He was running, but this time he was aware. He knew something more than he knew as a child. This stranger was there, waking him to his dreams.

*We ran in a single line in order to get through the debris. Riggs and Lee were in line behind me and had gotten trapped behind some fallen junk or got scared and stopped running because things were falling all around us.*

The Dream Maker was changing this dream. There was no longer that mindless, fearful running. Now Werner had other feelings—feelings which were becoming stronger than his fear of fire.

*I remember running on in the dream knowing that if I turned back all three of us would probably get trapped. This thought made me want to keep running. But suddenly I saw both their faces in front of me. I had this strong feeling inside of my chest. I felt confused. I wanted to run out. I knew I had to act. I knew I had to go back and find them. I knew I had to stop running.*
*I turned and felt very scared. The building was completely in flames. But this feeling inside my chest was so strong that it pushed me back through the fire. I don't remember what happened then, but I know somehow I got both of them out and we were all safe.*

The alarm clock was ringing as Werner finished the dream. He knew something had happened. It was almost as if someone had been talking to him all night. He tried to remember the dream but could only catch bits of it.

It was getting late. Werner got up to wash and shave. As he bent over and splashed the warm water on his face, he remembered more of the dream. *A fire in a hotel and running.* Werner felt good this morning—something in his dream left him feeling good. He liked that.

The dream feeling would not leave him; the Dream Maker had done his work well. In some ways Werner was in great danger. He would soon have to start running if he was to keep himself intact, if he was to remain the Werner he had been so long, the Werner who knew how to run. But the Dream Maker was there in his chest, weighing him down, making it harder to run. The Dream Maker had caught Werner doing what he always did—running. The dream faded but the feeling remained. Werner was trying to forget that for one of the first times in his life he had stopped running.

By the time he got to work, Werner was running again, darting inside of his head, fending off imaginary arguments, throwing reasons at all those people in his head. The staff finished work by 12:30 P.M. Dominic had asked us all to have lunch together, to take a little time. Nobody wanted to but Dominic insisted. We decided to have food sent in from the delicatessen a few streets over. By the time the deliveryman arrived, Werner was racing.

Almost everything Werner does makes sense. He is the director of research for our foundation. He thinks analytically and perspectively, constantly measuring things, but behind the brain-talk he is fragile. His soft features make him look delicate. In many ways he is fragile; he has epilepsy. Werner doesn't have seizures often, but when they come he looks as though all those people and things that he runs from had caught up with him. He looks beat up and bruised and helpless.

We talked over lunch and then Werner wanted to go. Dominic told him to wait for a few more moments. "Wait for what? I want to go."

The rest of us sat talking, but no one seemed to know what

to do. There was "something happening" but no one knew exactly what. We could see that Werner was running, but somehow it didn't make sense.

By the time we finished lunch Dominic told Werner, "You don't have to give in. You can, if you want, but you must choose what you know."

Werner didn't say anything to Dominic, but left immediately. He could be alone at home. He sifted through research papers, and with each page he got more and more tired. He tried to fight sleep. He had work to do, but his eyes and chest were heavy. The Dream Maker pressed down on Werner, making him sleep. The afternoon is a good time to sleep, especially when the house is quiet and empty and there seems to be too much work to do on the desk. Werner slept soundly. The Dream Maker was ready with more fire and more running than Werner had ever known.

*I am at the Center arguing with Dominic. As we fight a fire breaks out. The entire building is on fire. I start to run and Dominic grabs me. He won't let me go. I start screaming at him, "Dominic, Dominic, we'll be killed." I feel terrified. Dominic keeps holding me down. It's as if he weighs a thousand pounds. I struggle to get free. The more I try the sadder I get. I am afraid that I am going to be burned to death. Then I realize that I am not burning up. I ask Dominic what is happening, why aren't we burning up? He says, "There's no fire." I feel embarrassed and very sad. I finally realize that I made up the fire, that it wasn't real. I feel Dominic holding me. I begin to cry very deeply.*

Werner woke from the dream crying, remembering all the times he had run. He remembered the good reasons for running as a child and it made him sad to know that there had been no person to run to for comfort. He saw how he ran even now from his friends. He remembered his dream from the night before. Everything began to fit together. He knew that he didn't have to run; he knew there was some place to go; he knew there was a reason not to run. He could not stop crying and wishing, "If there had only been someone or some place to run to then." He remembered the dream—*Dominic*.

Werner called Dominic on the phone, "Dominic, help me." His words were so choked beneath his tears that he could barely talk. Werner told Dom the dream. Dominic knew what Werner was feeling, what he was running from and coming to.

"You don't have to keep running from yourself," he told him. Werner listened and realized that what he really feared was running from himself, and more than anything in his life he wanted to stay with himself.

We fear the Dream Maker and the pictures he brings because we fear fully entering the world he represents. Werner was afraid of *not* running. What would he be like if he stayed and faced reality? What would he feel? What would it be like if he began to use the fire for himself?

Like a chain being built link by link, the Dream Maker Tradition was being forged in our lives. There is only one way to learn the Tradition and that is to experience it. This book will teach you about your own Dream Maker world, but that is like being invited into a nightmare. Once you have gone too far it seems as if you have made a grave mistake and there is no way of getting back. There isn't.

TRY THIS. Notice that having Breakthru Dreams requires a special kind of "giving in"—giving in to your feelings. Also notice that Werner had to recognize the real differences between his life as a child and his life in the present. In Part Three you will be taught to recognize your past, present, and future as they appear in your dreams. For now, imagine that you are Werner; imagine how difficult it is to believe you don't have to keep running. Imagine how it would feel to stop running and just be with someone.

# 4
# More Dreams

✦ Good Eagle knew about dreams. He could sing all the medicine songs of the Dakotas. And he was singing now. He sat
in the cleansing teepee. The hot smoke and fires made all of
the warriors sweat. There was a trouble among the people;
Dancing Elk, the chief's only son, was sick.

For three days Good Eagle had been seeking a healing
dream. Each day he would cleanse himself and each night
he would sleep in the medicine teepee and wait for the
dream. None came. As dawn of the fourth morning broke
the dream came at last.

"All of our people are singing the songs of death. Dancing Elk has gone even before the time of running. And then
as the bravest of the warriors prepared to punish themselves for his death, there was a great roar, all the women of
the village began to wail. I too was wailing. In my shame to
hide my tears I ran away. An eagle flew around me and
said, 'Medicine man, do not cry like an old woman. Turn
your tears into a song.' I woke up singing this song:

> O ye people be ye healed,
> Life anew, bring into ye."

The song was the beginning of Dancing Elk's cure. Good
Eagle had found the Dream Maker Tradition. In later years
he continued to dream healing dreams for his people. He
became a great healer.

Indians lived in America when it was different. There was time for people to get together and celebrate or mourn or heal each other of their sicknesses. In their hearts they were open to the life around them. The Dakotas have gone but their dream tradition remains.

The Dream Maker was weaving a historical tapestry. As Riggs read and thought, he began to find clues that we were on to something very old and something very new. First Dom, then Werner—each one learning something new from his dreams, and then in turn learning something new in waking.

Werner and Dom met with Riggs and they often talked late into the night. They all knew that something was happening and that it would continue, but they did not know what it was.

It was already late fall and everything seemed "normal." But Riggs, Werner, and Dom were concerned. They all were applying more and more pressure to the other staff members. But nothing was happening; the pressure was building "underground" and someone was going to "crack" because of it.

## Lee—The Face of Insanity

Lee is a psychiatrist and the medical director at The Center Foundation. That day, in the large staff therapy room, Dr. Lee was more of a patient. While the rest of his friends and staff were having a group, he was drawing himself into the darkest corner. Lee didn't feel like participating; he couldn't identify the symptoms, but felt chilled and sick. He felt himself being pulled into a place or feeling from which he could not extricate himself. The group became fuzzy, far away; he could not see clearly anymore; he felt drugged.

LSD experiences had been like this for him. But that was before his internship when it was "hip" to be into drugs. Lee had matured. Nothing in his medical books prepared him for what he was experiencing.

Werner looked at Dominic. It was obvious who was breaking. Lee hadn't told anyone but he had begun his initiation into the world of the Dream Maker. He had had a dream, a nightmare, which he didn't tell anyone but which would not leave him.

Dominic walked over to Riggs who shook his head no and said, "Let Werner help him. He needs to live out of what he knows." Dom motioned to Werner.

"Shit," Werner thought, "I don't know what to do. I wish Riggs or Dom would do something." He looked back across the room; they looked back at him. Lee was obviously breaking up and needed help. Werner took a breath and walked over to Lee. "What do you want? You look like you could use some help."

"Maybe I do, maybe I don't. You can go fuck yourself, you're shaking, you're so fucking scared." Werner was frozen; he didn't know what to do. Help was supposed to be accepted, but Lee wasn't making it easy.

The Dream Maker was there. Just as he created dream pictures he showed Werner how to act and live now in a new way. "Lee, look at me. I want you to tell me what has been happening to you." Lee could barely hear Werner's words, but he knew the sound of Werner's voice had changed. He couldn't help but answer.

"Werner, I had a nightmare two days ago and it won't leave me alone; it keeps haunting me."

"What is it?"


*I was in a living room and as the phone rang I had the realization that I was dreaming, but also afraid that the words the person on the phone was going to say could be magic, they could kill me.*


Lee drew further into the corner. His eyes were bulging and engorged. The line between dreaming and waking was no longer distinct.

"Lee, I want you to keep talking to me. Tell me more about the dream." Werner was there trying to draw the Dream Maker into the open.

---

*I picked up the receiver and I think it was my father. He said just a few words, and then began to say some mumbled sounds that I immediately recognized as the words that could kill me.*

The dream faded and Lee recalled his last visit home. His father was dying of cancer. At times when he was at home taking short walks with his father, they were able to say things to one another that they were never able to say before. His father had told him a dream that had deeply touched them both.

*I dreamt it was my last few hours and there were many things I wanted to say or hadn't said; and now it was too late.*

They walked and talked and shared tears that they had never shown before. In the final days there were moments of real sharing. But then Lee's father would retreat to old distant ways of acting and Lee would become torn between really being himself and waiting for it all to pass.

During the waiting came the nightmare. Werner brought him back from his reverie and prodded him to remember more of the dream. Lee could barely speak.

*I quickly pulled the phone away, thinking that it couldn't kill me unless I heard it all, but I underestimated their effect on me. I felt a terrible, powerful sensation in my body, as though I were getting smaller and more compact, being compressed by something outside of me and being sucked into the phone. Things were getting black, darker than I have ever seen before. I felt as if I were going to die.*

The uncontrolled emotions from Lee's unconscious battered his conscious mind. There was no longer a balance; the Dream Censor was overthrown but the Dream Maker was not in control. It was a violent balance Werner was working with.

Lee was awake and asleep, dreaming and awake. For the

first time in his life he was totally experiencing how his life diminished each time he allowed himself to hold back all that he knew. There was so much more he had wanted to say to his father. Werner was passing the Dream Maker Tradition on to Lee. But first Lee would have to go through this experience and live from it.

Unlike Freud and Jung there was no distance between Lee and Werner. There was no interpretation that would have helped change this dream from a symbolic message to a transformative experience. Lee's dream was not a Breakthru Dream, but it was a beginning. It was another movement toward Dream Maker Awareness. Lee was not having a dream, he was having a Dream Maker awakening. Werner got him to stand up.

This was the time and this was the place. The Dream Maker was here in waking. Riggs, Dominic, and Werner had begun to get everyone. They weren't getting after people, they were showing the way. They were feeling at a different level than the rest of the staff. That created a vortex that was sweeping everyone down, into what we did not know.

There was no glitter or Hollywood glamour in that therapy room in Los Angeles, only people. Each one educated and yet each wondering what it was they were witnessing. They had all heard about what Riggs had done with Dominic, and Dominic had told his dreams. But now they were seeing it. This Dream Maker seemed like a presence, an entity. The room was alive with the sense that we had only seen part of what was going to happen.

Lee felt wobbly. What was happening and going to happen had occurred before. This was not new for the Dream Maker; it was only new for those who sat in the room and participated for the first time.

With the Indians of North America, the ancient Greeks of Aesculaepius, and the Senoi of Malaysia—where there had been groups of people working together—the Dream Maker had become visible. He rarely comes to one person alone. Because often if he does—the person is overwhelmed by feeling. The

Dream Maker needs many dreamers who can help each other to grow.

Here in this leaderless group the Dream Maker would be the leader. He would awaken the Dream Maker in each and make him take responsibility. Like a dream, the happenings in the room unfolded . . .

Werner was whispering something to Lee whose crying twisted and convulsed his body. Each time Werner whispered, Lee's body would double up with sobs. The staff was frozen, waiting. Something was happening. They were all good psychologists, but they were not Dream Makers. And this was not the time for just therapy.

Werner bent over Lee and whispered, "You have to give it up, Lee. You have to let go of all those thoughts and intellectual games. It is time for you to wake up. Open your eyes to how you feel; your life is passing you by."

Werner's words evoked a memory for Lee. He remembered a dream that he had let go by. A dream of his own awakening.

*Werner, I had this dream. I don't know—maybe a week or two ago. I forgot it until just now. I dreamt I saw a little boy who has a third eye. He was crying because he had this eye. I told him not to be afraid, it was okay. I had one too, but it was covered up.*

As Lee told the dream, he cried more and more; he was afraid of his own awakening. The dream had made it clear enough: what he knew and saw as a child, Lee covered up. But now it was the time to uncover, to see and feel all that he could. Werner did not wait until the next dream or the next time; he pushed Lee to complete the dream now. "Lee, I want you to open your eyes. I want you to see everything that you can see."

Lee's eyes were full and sad; he was afraid to really see. Werner touched his eyes; Lee shuddered. He seemed so afraid, so delicate. Werner made him ask others to touch his eyes, to see his eyes. It was a community dream with Lee talking and telling each person what he saw.

As he spoke, it was with a vulnerable authority. He was a dream character to everyone else. He didn't talk about what people did right and wrong; he talked to them about them and himself. He could see; his eyes were full of tears.

He told them about himself. "I feel like I am a huge fire. When I don't live with as much as I can, I don't feel really alive. I want you all to know that I am going to die. I am not going to live forever. I want everything that I can have. I want every one of my feelings."

As the staff sat there together we knew each other. We had been acquainted for years, but now we knew each other fully. Riggs, Dominic, and Werner were no longer intimate strangers; they were our friends. We sat together and cried and talked. Each of us aware of something new. We had all begun to change, to move into our own personal initiation toward becoming Dream Makers. We didn't know what to call what was happening, but we felt it.

The Dream Maker looked out of all those crying eyes, looking into the eyes of each person for a sign. Dominic, Werner, Riggs, and Lee, their dreams were visionary and insane. Everyone sat there looking at one another—some afraid to see what they had seen. Some were afraid of the insanity, others were afraid of the sanity. The Dream Maker inside each person feared nothing; it wanted everything.


Joe and Riggs had taken a long drive to the beach with their families. They couldn't quite rationally understand what had happened the other day. Riggs related the experience to the Western Indians and to Eastern Satori experiences.

But Joe wasn't really listening. He didn't have a dream. He felt afraid. He thought to himself, "I won't be able to do it." Riggs and Joe talked but Joe didn't really let his thoughts and feelings all out. He didn't let Riggs know how afraid he really was.

Riggs changed the point of conversation to how someone outside of the therapy could use his dreams in the same way. "Joe, don't you see. You don't have to be in therapy to get more from your dreams. What therapy does is intensify your dreams. Therapy and dreams set up a dynamic which is too powerful for the way most people live. But when someone is smart enough to know they want to change, all that they have to do is tap into their dreams." Riggs talked on and on about what it was possible for a person to get without therapy. But Joe wasn't really listening; he was preoccupied with what was happening to himself.

TEST YOURSELF AGAIN. You must want something to be reading this book, but what? Have you really let yourself know what you would like from it? Do it now—ask yourself the following questions; if you can answer yes to one of them you are ready for Dream Maker Awareness: 1) Do I really want to change my life? 2) Do I want something more with the people I know? 3) Am I willing to feel more even if the feelings won't all be pleasant and easy?

Things happen fast here in California. It seems if something new is going to emerge it will be here. Yet beneath the fast-changing exterior there is a deep-down skepticism. Everyone wants to know, "What's your bag, what's your trick?" Without ever showing its true nature, California—and especially Los Angeles—is very conservative.

There have been too many quick cures, weekend miracles, and overnight stars. The staff at the Center were paid skeptics. They didn't believe all the PR hypes and yet here inside their own clinic something was happening.

That something was trying to spread its influence at the Center, and at times it seemed as if it might. But then after a Breakthru Dream had become little more than a memory, the staff would be divided as to what direction we should take.

What the Dream Maker had accomplished over the last year was in jeopardy. Joe, Jerry, Steve, and Carole had strong opinions—mostly against working more with dreams. If they stayed completely set, it could mean the breakup of the Center or the end of the dream explorations.

The staff sat in the conference room. The sign outside the door read Staff Only. As the secretary passed she could hear loud shouting. "This isn't some council meeting of Indians or some voodoo rite. I want to get down to business."

Joe was very angry with Dominic. Dominic said, "Listen Joe, all I want to do is have a dream group once a week. We don't want to do anything more than talk about our dreams. We think they are really important."

"I don't want to. I've studied and trained to be a therapist. I don't like these dreamy changes."

Jerry butted in, "You know I don't agree with all that psychoanalytic interpretation."

Riggs interrupted, "That's not what Dominic means. We think there is a new kind of dream emerging among us. I've looked all through the literature and what is happening in our dreams just isn't discussed. I really think we're on to something important."

Lee added, "Joe, you know what a skeptic I am, but I really believe in what I experienced. It was as if my dreams broke through defenses I just wasn't getting to in therapy."

Jerry was furious, "You see what I mean. It begins to sound like magic, or shamanism, or who knows what."

Jerry went on, loudly, "You keep talking about this new experience, about waking up while you are dreaming, about your dreams giving you a new reference point. I don't believe it."

Lee asked him, "Do you believe that I am changing?"

"Yes, I do—but so am I."

Lee said, "That's just the point. We aren't talking about replacing therapy; we just want to add to what we are already doing."

Everyone was quiet and then Riggs spoke. "Magic—that's not a bad word, Jerry." He looked at Jerry and continued, "Therapy really seems like magic sometimes, and this new kind of dream we are talking about is like a natural magic."

Riggs went on, "You know, when you take all the mysticism and beliefs away from shamanism and Satori you just have good people having breakthrough experiences. Their experiences give them a new awareness that needs to be lived to be maintained. This dream we are talking about is like that. Just the way meaningful therapy experiences are like that. But it happens at night."

For Joe, all he knew was that he felt pressure to change. He felt unsettled by it. No one was asking him to say or do anything radically different. But he could sense it, something coming inside of himself. The staff was divided and taking sides; it seemed like a miniwar. The meeting brought no resolutions. Joe held fast—the four who wanted to work with dreams went out to lunch after the meeting.

"I'm not worried—it's all content—I think we're just now getting down to the nitty-gritty." Werner seemed so sure. If anyone should have been scared it was Werner, but he was so sure.

"Jesus, Werner, I'm not sure," Lee said. "I don't know what all this is leading to. What if someone freaks out and doesn't come out of it?"

"Wait a minute," Dom was getting mad with Lee. "We aren't exactly in the safe and sane business. We've got to take chances, push to the limits."

Even the four dreamers could not agree. No one could say exactly what to do or what would come of it.

✦  It was a hard time for Nakasuk. He was seeking his rite to manhood but he was afraid. His older brother told him that he must go out and hunt the seal by himself. Nakasuk was scared. The women of the village were beginning to look at him in strange ways. The other boys his age had already done this deed. He was the last one. And now was the time. It must be done before the summer's end.

The snow was a flat white. Nakasuk pressed his body close to it. Seeking protection from it. All of his life he had learned to respect the snow, ice, and water. The great white bear was very close. Closer than was good, unless Nakasuk was trying to sink the killing spear. He was not.

For two days Nakasuk had been hunting seal in this new hunting place that he had found. He had two good catches when he first saw the great bear. This was the bear's favorite hunting spot and his keen nose told him something was different. The bear did not think. He only knew to react. He stood up. Nakasuk pressed closer to the snow. The flat snow reflected no unusual movement. The bear settled to the task of seal hunting. His huge body slipped into the icy water.

Nakasuk returned to his sled and dogs. It would be a good time for returning. He yelled at the dogs; they did not want to come out of their protected snow valley Nakasuk had found to camp in. But the sound of their master's strong voice sent them into action. The sled was rigged and the seal catch would soon be loaded and Nakasuk would be on his way. The mush home was a good one but there was a heaviness within Nakasuk's heart.

Even after his return to the village Nakasuk could not find relief from the heaviness. Everyone praised him. Something else was weighing his heart down. The weariness of the journey slowly overtook him and he slept.

"The great bear is chasing me. I do not know what to do. I run but there is no freedom from his chasing."

As he dreamt Nakasuk began to awaken in his dream. He was awake and aware that this was a dream. He could feel the fear inside his body.

"The bear came closer and closer. I ran to the edge of the water. I was afraid. I knew I would perish if I went into it and I knew the bear would kill me. I turned to fight the bear. I could hear the mocking voices of the women of the tribe telling me I would be killed. I decided to fight. I took my spear and raised it. The bear stopped and no longer was it a bear but puppies. I had found a new team of wonderful dogs. My heart was full and happy."

Nakasuk woke with gladness. His family was happy to see a change in their son. They had worried that the rite had made him sullen. But now their Nakasuk was back. He told them of his dream and his father spoke of "this great dream."

His father said, "Nakasuk, you have dreamt the dreams of a wise one. I shall tell the elders of what dream power you have."

The Eskimo boy was becoming a shaman. Very few men were called to this duty and Nakasuk was to become one. As he grew into manhood he learned to understand the secret teaching of dreams. He cured his people of many illnesses with his dreams. He brought back magic words that helped his people to feel better. He knew that many times the outside spirits of great fear were the same as the inside spirits. He taught his people and they were happy under his leadership.

# Joe—L.A.

Los Angeles is not Tibet or Japan or any other exotic place. Joe had studied about every exotic place in the world. He read about great Zen masters and Tibetan monks and yogis, but he could never quite believe in any of them who came to America.

Joe wanted to believe—early in his career he had written a book with a chapter called "Beyond Psychotherapy." But that had all been theory; he had never found that road himself; he never could go beyond. It frightened him now when he saw that some of his colleagues were changing. They weren't just a little changed; they were transformed. They talked confidently and deeply; they acted spontaneously and flowingly. No matter what, Joe knew he could talk to Riggs. He went over to see him.

Riggs had company, one of his trainee therapists. "Okay, Alan, that about wraps up this session. I think your patient is doing fine; all that I want you to work on is keeping her in touch with her body." Alan visited for a while and left. Joe waited until Alan was gone.

"Riggs, I'm upset with what went on in the staff meeting yesterday. Look, we've learned to be individuals, to make it on our own. Shit, the way you guys were talking I start to think of us as some kind of Indian tribe."

Riggs said, "Joe, I get tired of being a professional. Hell, psychiatrists, psychologists, and counselors seem crazier than almost everyone. I want something more. I feel more like an archeologist than a psychologist."

"Joe, my dreams have really begun to change. It is almost as if there was a person or a thing or a new state of consciousness in my dreams. I can't put my finger on it but something new is happening. I have a hunch that it won't come full circle until everyone knows it for themselves. It's a very strong hunch and I think it will really come true for us. I don't know how, but it will."

Riggs kept talking and then realized he was talking to himself. Joe's attention wasn't on Riggs. Joe began to get up. "Relax, Joe. Sit back and relax."

Joe quipped back, "Great advice to give, but who can follow it?"

Riggs was standing there not saying anything. "You can, Joe. You can sit down and tell me how you are feeling."

Joe's face got very red and his eyes watered. Riggs was younger than he was, but now he felt as if Riggs was a hundred years old. He talked to him, and he felt like a child.

"Joe, don't try to solve your problems. Your feelings and sadness are not a problem." Joe's large back was heaving with his soft crying. He spent the afternoon on Riggs's couch, talking about how he felt.

Joe left Riggs's about 6:30 P.M. and went home. Gina, his wife, cooked a Persian dish with some exotic pancakes. They laughed and had a good time with their little girl, Kedra, but Joe was still puzzled from his talk. He knew Riggs was different, and that he was saying something to him. He suspected Riggs was trying to pull him over into a world which was familiar and yet strange. What he didn't suspect was how. Their talk had seemed like any other talk, but it wasn't.

The Dream Maker was there. The Dream Maker wasn't going to let this group splinter apart; they had been together too long—come too far—to not take the final step. The Dream

Maker knew if he could just push Joe over the edge, make him an ally, instead of an enemy, he would have a permanent home.

Joe was difficult to crack. He had tried large doses of LSD and still remained collected. Some of the only times he really cracked was when Riggs pinned him down and made him admit that he was alive and in need of deeper contact. Like a team of surgeons, Riggs and the Dream Maker worked on Joe—Riggs softening him up during the day and the Dream Maker ready with the night.

It was early when Joe and Gina went to bed. They wanted to make love. They had been married for many years and had recently gone through a real marital crisis, and now, both approaching forty, they were laughing like teen-agers. They touched and laughed. Getting more and more excited, Gina pressed her body closer to Joe's; she felt so alive. She loved sex and Joe loved her. They were getting to know each other in different ways.

As Joe slept, the Dream Maker made his way into his room. The Dream Maker was creating a dream by using Joe's memories of the Oregon woods to tell Joe what he had to do.

*Up in the woods. I go into a new little town. There is a lodge by the side of the river. The river is very strong and wide. I want to cross very badly. I feel my body is alive. I know I can be pulled across. I talk about what I know with Riggs, and we decide to do it. When we reach the lodge, right away I get into the water. It is very cold. I get scared: the current is stronger than I thought it would be. The river is roaring. It is so loud I cannot hear anything. I am afraid I am going to drown. I never felt anything so powerful. I don't know what to do. I am starting to be pulled under. Then I feel this tremendous grip on my arm. Riggs is there. He has my arm. We begin to go across together. He teaches me how to pull him. We take turns pulling each other across. We are more powerful than the river. As we stand on the other side we see other people trying to cross by themselves. Jerry tried and can't make it. Carole tries and nearly hits the rocks. I can tell immediately who will be able to do it and who won't. They have to both try for themselves and be pulled.*

The Dream Maker let that dream settle into Joe's sleep. But tonight the Dream Maker would not leave quickly. As Joe left the dream, he slept even more heavily, sinking into a deeper state of sleep. As the night progressed the Dream Maker wove another dream. This time a dream that would teach Joe what to do.

*I am in the woods. I recognize this river. I want to cross. It is very large and powerful. I know that I have crossed it before. I plunge in. I see Riggs on the far bank. The river engulfs me and pulls me into the middle. It is impossible to go in either direction. I feel like I am going to drown. And then Riggs shouts to me, "Go easy." I stop trying to swim. I begin to go easy and the river takes me to the shore where Riggs is standing. I get up. We have command over the river.*

It was early, before daylight, as the Dream Maker stole from Joe's room. He stopped and listened for Kedra's ten-year-old dreams. He would return to her later—when she was older. He had done his work tonight. (Children regularly dream Breakthru Dreams up until about age twelve, when their dreams become normalized. However, in a few cultures which cultivate the Dream Maker Approach, such as the Senoi of Malaysia, children continue to dream naturally as they mature. Their dreams, like their bodies, grow larger and stronger.)

Joe sat up in bed, smiling. The words "Go easy" played on his lips. *Go easy*—he turned on the light. He turned the words *Go easy* around—his smile broadened. He felt a relief, a lightness. He knew what he had been fighting was his own personal fight; it didn't have anything to do with staff meetings and arguments.

The Dream Maker had changed his method. The figure—the teacher in the dreams—was no longer so mysterious. Slowly the Dream Maker was teaching us to teach each other in and from our dreams. We all were destined to become night travelers and teachers. But that is really jumping ahead; there were more crises to follow.

Like a grandfather who teaches each of his grandchildren something different, the Dream Maker had taught five of us. This new age we were entering was more powerful than the one we had come from. As we grew, we shared what we knew, teaching each other what we had learned from our dreams. The Dream Maker was now ready to teach another step, to take us to another part of the Dream Maker Tradition, a part we would each have to learn.

Joe had begun to teach each one of us how to "go easy." Dominic, Werner, Riggs, and Lee understood, but not Jerry, Carole, or Steve; they were going in the opposite direction. Jerry was getting angry all the time. He would drive himself into a frenzy with thoughts that plagued him. The Dream Maker was getting Jerry ready.

Over and over Jerry would wind up storming about how his thoughts were destroying his life. But somehow, with therapy and all, he was still not realizing what was happening to him. The Dream Maker knew what to do.

## Jerry—The Boston Tornado

If anyone in the world knew how to avoid going easy it was Jerry. Jerry is one of those people who dragged himself up from the worst. He grew up in the Jewish slums of Boston. He was a thug with a heart as large as the moon; it was too bad he lived on the dark side so long.

Well, that was then. He had left home at eighteen and became an educated young man. He was filled with drive—an insatiable drive. As he got older, he began to realize the drive worked both for him and against him. It had gotten him educated, but when he was feeling bad he turned all his energy against himself.

Retrospectively, you could say Jerry felt betrayed. Joe had been his strongest ally and now Joe didn't argue anymore; he smiled and took it easy. Jerry felt like exploding. The weeks had passed since Joe "knew" what it really meant to "go easy." He had begun teaching us to slow down and, in turn, he took in what each of us had to teach.

Jerry was having trouble learning to go easy. Lee had just given him a therapy session in which he had been criticized very heavily. Lee reprimanded him on trading in his body sensations for thoughts. He fought what Lee said; the Dream Maker coiled in his brain. That night, as he slept, the Dream Maker would be within striking distance.

Jerry had trouble falling asleep. He kept thinking about the way he fought everyone around him. But he could not fight away the Dream Maker.

*I've got this machine-gun type weapon, and I'm roaming our neighborhood wiping out people. Actually, the gun fires my thoughts at them, and it releases my thoughts in a flood of water. So, I'm really washing out these people. They disappear when I press the trigger; I get rid of them. In my dream they are people who don't "matter" to me. I feel myself angry and then satisfied every time I wipe out a person.*

*Next, I'm running into Riggs's house. I know what I have done; I have murdered people. I think that for sure I will be caught and certainly imprisoned or gassed or electrocuted. I want to commit suicide so I won't be caught. I tell Riggs, "I've just killed a whole bunch of people. I washed them out with this gun. I killed them." Then I see that my friend, Bob Amico, is with Riggs and that they are chatting. I begin screaming at them in a frenzy, "I want you to hate me. I want you to hate me. I want you to hate me."*

*Riggs just looks at me calmly, peacefully, softly and says, "I just feel sad looking at you." No matter how intensely and loudly I scream at him, he just says the same thing over and over.*

*I'm more frenzied now, yelling louder at them, clutching the*

*gun. I aim it at them while I'm screaming. I pull the trigger . . . a*
*large blobby drop of thought lazily falls out of the muzzle onto the*
*floor. I look at them. Riggs is still saying, "I feel sad looking at*
*you." I feel a powerful sorrow inside my chest, and burst into sobs.*
*I cry out to Riggs, "Help me." I can't wipe him out with my*
*thoughts. "Help me. Help me, Riggs."*

This dream brought Jerry a new realization. As he rolled
over in bed, he started laughing. It all seemed so clear—so
easy—what Riggs said, what Dom said, and Lee and Werner
and Joe. "God," he thought, "I've been so close all this time.
They know, they really know." His eyes felt heavy and sad and
glad.

He thought about how he fought with Lee. It seemed so ridiculous. Jerry remembered some of the things he had said to
Lee—"It's just your thoughts about my thoughts"—and then the
dream pictures would return bringing with them the dream feelings.

The Dream Maker had changed his method. Now the
dreams were like giant messages; there wasn't anything mysterious. We had gone deep enough into the dreams to take away all
the mystery. Now they revealed to us exactly what we needed.

For Jerry the Dream Maker had taken his waking defenses
and crushed them with a dream. The defenses seemed childish
and unreasonable. He didn't need a therapy session or a therapist to tell him what it meant. He knew.

TRY THIS: Think about the words that Joe and Jerry received in their dreams, "Go easy" and "Help me." In Part
Three, Day 20, we will teach you to find your own Dream
Maker words, words you can use to change how you feel in
your life. For now use Joe's words and Jerry's words. Imagine what it would be like for you to live an hour or a day or
a week from a "Go easy" awareness or a "Help me" awareness.

# 6
# More Dream Makers

The Dream Maker Tradition was coming out of its infancy at the Center. What was happening was previewed theoretically by Dr. James Hillman, the Jungian analyst, when he wrote: "The myth of analysis will give way to a new myth. From Apollonian to Dionysian, from rational to emotional, from individual to group." It was almost as if he had anticipated what was happening to us. The theories and practices we had developed about feelings and waking were extending into the night and into dreams.

For most of the staff it was no longer just theory; we were changing, giving up the old roles of doctors, rediscovering the Dream Maker Tradition and becoming more and more a modern-day community.

Jerry was changed to our amazement. He finally wasn't taking his thoughts so seriously. Like the laughing Buddha, he had found one of the most pleasant secrets of life. He taught us that, "Thoughts, like dreams, are pictures of life; never take your thoughts as seriously as your feelings." He was a Dream Maker; he knew real truths and taught them.

## Steve—The Fear of Freedom

Next to Los Angeles there is the Pacific Ocean. Steve would take long walks along the beach and think about what was happening. He was one of the founding therapists, but didn't feel like he was finding his home; he felt as if he was losing it, afraid of the power and excitement he saw all around him, left out.

If every person has a basic fear, it is the fear of freedom. Steve was no different. He had been raised in a traditional Jewish family. He was a man, but something had been taken out of him. He was a psychologist and a good therapist, but his life somehow had yet to become exciting and dynamic.

Something was missing, as if something had been stolen from him. His parents were not child beaters, but we often thought he might have been better off if they had been. They had verbally beaten him, over the years of growing up. His parents had lost a boy and he had lost something of himself.

A beautiful and active boy was molded into a miniature adult; he became at an early age part nonathletic father and part bitchy mother. Stephen David—all he knew was to doubt himself and what was happening. "It is all too much for me. I don't know what is happening around home, but things are going too fast for me. I don't want to get to know everything." And then he would stutter. It was as if his life would stumble when he stuttered. His words would catch in his throat.

Joe worked with Steve, time and again, bringing him out of his past and to the edge of freedom, but he could not seem to make the transition. He could not accept that he had within his grasp the freedom to be himself. Back and forth he went, coming out and then retreating to a nowhere land in which he was lost to himself in daze and confusion. He wasn't just crazy then, he was lost.

Like so many people who taste freedom in themselves or with other people, Steve kept letting it slip away. That was Steve's insanity.

It was early April and all the therapists had gone away together for a two-week camping trip in the desert. This was a time that we took just for ourselves, to be with each other. Nothing special—just no interruptions.

The desert was beginning to warm up after a cool winter . . . in that in-between place of hot and cold. It was night and Steve slept with Carole. He looked as if he had found something new in his life; he and Carole fit together. They talked; her softness and caring was something new for him.

The next morning as we sat around having coffee and exchanging dreams, Steve was taking a greater part. His responses were more gutsy. We talked and shared our dreams until just before noon. We all knew Steve was getting close to understanding what it meant to be a Dream Maker.

Like a teasing showgirl, the Dream Maker brought hope to Steve and then withdrew, leaving him standing without anything to say or do, leaving him with the choice to take another step. The sunset was a long way away. We hiked and rode our dirt bikes. It was sunset before we stopped.

The desert at night was a natural place for the Dream Maker to come alive. The desert was alive and scary. We built a big fire and talked. We had had a good day of riding our bikes down sand washes—all of us, that is, except Steve. He hung back. He had "come out" in the morning and then withdrawn. He had wanted to go on this trip and then he wanted it to end.

Riggs and Werner were talking about flying down the sand dunes. Steve moped. In between the spaces of the talk, the night came closer. Steve was retreating—away from the fire, away from the talk, closer to the night. We didn't notice.

It was late; Steve had gone to bed. A few of us sat up talking, but now no longer of motorcycles. We talked of the changes we were going through, how precarious life seemed as we sat on this spinning globe. We all had that fearful excitement that comes from talking late into the night. We were beginning to formulate what it meant to be a Dream Maker.

Jerry was coming into his own. He was talking to Riggs, Lee, and Dom. "When a person takes a step, takes a new direction in his life, then the dream process will change. You see, a dream teaches you the direction of your life; it shows you your defenses against that direction, and it shows you the images that you use to fool yourself."

Dom blurted out, "Everyone has the power to make his dreams. We aren't dreaming dreams anymore: we are becoming makers of dreams."

We were really excited. It must have been around 2:30 or 3:00 A.M. when we first heard the sound. If you have ever camped in the desert, you can imagine how scared we got; it was a gurgling sound.

Riggs jumped out of his chair, "God, what was that?" Jerry got up. We listened again and heard the same gurgling sound, a raspy choking sound. We were frozen; the goose bumps ran up and down our spines.

Jerry asked Lee to put some more wood on the fire. As it blazed we could see the outlines of Steve's body, sleeping about fifty feet away. The primitive sound was coming out of him. Jerry hurried over.

Steve looked about six with his tense body, messy curly hair, and a little saliva running down his cheek. Jerry began to wake Steve, to let the dream feelings out that the Dream Maker had created.

*I dreamt my mother was talking to me, yelling at me until I was completely wiped out. I walked over to a window and began staring out. I could feel my throat. I was trying to talk and I couldn't. I was numbed out and paralyzed. I felt as if I was locked inside.*

Jerry helped him to let the dream awareness take over. What was important was the feeling in his body that he had carried over from childhood. It was frightening—to be there in the middle of the desert in the night while one of our friends fought with a past that was limiting his present.

Steve was choking. Tears were running down Jerry's face as

he helped him survive the nightmare. He was facing it, feeling, not running from it. And there with Jerry he was coming once again to the edge of his freedom. Jerry helped him for two hours. The darkness was filled with the sounds of a boy choking, wanting more, but having only his insanely normal parents to model after. Steve was going through the scariest experience of his life. Jerry helped him drift back into the sweet sleep of someone who is surrounded by people who love him and protect him.

The rest of us sat around talking. We had taken another step; we knew that we would not slip backwards again. We would take these little steps together, helping each other.

Jerry was really moved by what had happened. Later Dominic and Lee sat him between them and talked to him for over an hour. He was crying, sobbing, from his chest.

No one moved until ten-thirty the next morning. The sun had long since taken away the coolness of the night. Steve was up and around, making coffee and rousing everyone. He was talking at a fast pace, telling us a dream he had.

*I was camping in the mountains with a whole group of friends. Most people were just lying around doing nothing. Others were sitting around a burnt-out campfire, probably from the night before. I remember getting bored. I began to get edgy wanting everybody to get up and do something active and exciting. Nobody seemed to care, much less do anything. Finally, I couldn't stand it any longer. I began to turn the camp upside down—literally that—I was turning everything, sleeping bags with people in them, camp chairs, tents, upside down. I felt strong in showing everyone how I felt. I remember Lee in my dream. Watching me. It felt good seeing him. After I turned the camp upside down, I walked up to Carole. She and I knew we loved each other. I went a little distance and watched my friends. They liked what I had done.*

We were all watching Steve. He had turned the camp upside down. He was changed. Joe then told of his dream.

*I dreamt that I had found the answer to adulthood. I was talking to someone. The answer I explained was to live in the present. To keep talking.*

It all seemed so simple—and then so difficult. We knew we had found each other. Then Steve told us another dream.

*I was in a car that was sliding like butter through fences and walls of all different shapes and sizes. I remember trying to brake but the brakes wouldn't work. Actually braking only acted to increase the amount of sliding. I was a little scared in the dream, but mostly excited. I felt like I was going with the car rather than trying to oppose it. It was kind of exciting breaking things up.*

As Steve talked and told us his dreams, he seemed to be telling about all of us. The brakes were off; we had really begun to interfere with each other's lives even more. We knew that the dreams were a way for each of us to allow his walls and fences to be broken down. We were all excited and scared. The fear of freedom was passing. We had found, through our friends, the answer to adulthood. Not a single answer, but a living one.

## Carole—Finding the Brakes

Everyone was excited about Steve's changes—except Carole; it thrilled her and it scared her. She didn't know what was going to happen to their relationship. Everyone noticed it— after Steve's big breakthrough she was just a little quieter, a little more withdrawn. She had everything she ever wanted and now she would have to feel that she had it. As we packed to go home, Carole was torn. She didn't want to go back to more therapy. Lately, doing therapy had begun to really make the therapists open up more. Carole was trying to hold on to herself, trying to stop what she felt inside.

Carole—Lita as Steve had begun to call her—sat in the four-wheel drive station wagon. She felt angry and depressed; she didn't know how to enjoy so much feeling. Perhaps one of the most frightening things that can happen to a person is to find his or her direction in life, and for Lita that was happening. She had found Steve and now the life she always thought that she could have was happening.

Everyone thinks it surprising when a rock star commits suicide at the height of a career, but it really isn't. What does a person who has been trained all his life to "try and get ahead" do when there is no place left *to get to?* Lita was feeling more than she could believe. She felt different than the others on the staff; she was afraid to make the kind of moves they were making and still she was being dragged along in this powerful current we had tapped.

When you work in a group, you learn to live with the fact that everyone does not change at the same rate. That, of course, is easy for everyone to accept except the person who is not changing at the speed he thinks he should be. Well, Lita didn't like the way she was, but that wasn't so different for her. As she was growing up with three brothers, she learned to be rough and tumble. She was the biggest girl in her class and of Polish descent. The other children knew what to call her, "dumb Polack," how to make her feel the way she felt inside.

Lita grew up reading in her room, alone. It is sad to think how parents, brothers, and school can take a wonderful girl and make her feel big and ugly. Lita is beautiful and sensuous, simple and pleasing, but when she starts to feel bad and stops talking, she tells herself she is dumb—a dumb Polack.

She developed a secret world which, whenever she needed it, she would retreat to. Most people have them, but Lita didn't really want hers; she wanted to be herself, to have her body. That was hard since she had learned so many ugly things to label her body sensations.

Well, Lita began to retreat from the changes. She talked

and helped and worked, but she was distant, distrusting in a secret kind of way, and then she went through a period in which her secret world was revealed.

As she compared herself in her head to other people and their Breakthru Dreams and all the drama, she came up short. From the time she was twelve until she was twenty-four, she had not remembered any dreams at all. During the last few years she had begun remembering more and more. But now as she was trying harder and harder to keep up, she could remember nothing—not even a fragment. The less she remembered, the harder she got on herself, and the more she retreated.

Joe and Lee had been working with her, but she couldn't seem to get through it. Joe would give her intense sessions trying to help her feel her body. He kept helping her know that there was no one to keep up with, that she had to feel for herself what she was like, that she was enough.

It seemed like she had no luck. But Joe knew and Lee knew that she would break; it was just a matter of time before it happened. It had been over three months; time seemed to stand still for Lita. As everyone was getting closer, she retreated into her world, alone.

Except for the Dream Maker. Lita retreated from the waking world of talking into the world of thoughts and fantasies. She became a bomb that needed to explode.

Each dream that the Dream Maker sent Lita, she found ways of forgetting. No matter what the story, no matter how dramatic, she found ways of forgetting. The Dream Maker will do what he needs to do to make a person remember. Joe and Lee kept the pressure on from the outside. And the Dream Maker began to formulate particular kinds of dreams that Lita had not had before: body dreams, dreams that were organic, dreams that were in her bones and skin and blood, dreams that she could not forget.

The first dream she had was the beginning of a series of body dreams—dreams that told her how to find her way back into her body. She told Joe the dream during one of her sessions.

*I was aware of my body. There were big holes one-and-a-half inches deep covering my entire body, especially in my legs. They were filled up with flaky material, similar to pie crust. I knew it was dead; underneath was pink sensitive skin. I couldn't understand why it was there. I felt confused. I knew I wanted to put back slightly new material to replace the pie crust—new stuff that was all my own.*

As she told the dream, she withdrew. Joe asked her if she wanted to come out of the secret world. She was tentative, "Yes and no."

He said, "If you want to come out, then you have to finish the dream."

Lita's voice cracked, "Joe, I don't think I can. I mean, I'm not real smart. I don't know how."

He said, "The first step is to ask how."

Lita wasn't going to remain locked inside this time. She said, "Joe, how do I do it?"

"You have to touch the holes. You have to feel them, get to know them. You have to show them to me. Let me see you as you really are."

She began to press different spots on her legs. Each spot she touched brought more tears. She was tender—she was Lita—not dumb and quiet. The more she touched, the more her past surged up from her memory. Memories came—not pictures, but body memories. Lita was hurt. There was no secret world, only hurts. Lots of them—little ones and big ones, and as a child all she could do was hold them in. The more she touched, the more she began to feel what she had been doing to herself in the present.

"Joe," she whispered. "I don't want to do these things to myself anymore. I want to feel how sensitive and tender I really am."

Lita, the recluse, was becoming a person. Joe worked with her for over three hours. There was no place for secrets. She told of the little things she hid in order to keep herself crusted over.

TRY THIS: Notice that Lita's dream was about her body. Her dream told her how she felt and what she was missing in her body. In Part Three we will tell you how to ask questions which elicit the body feelings in your dreams. Until then do this: make up a dream about your body. What would you use to represent how your body feels? Is your made-up dream beautiful and satisfying? How do you show, in your made-up dream, what you don't like about your body?

Lita went through two hellish weeks trying to keep those tender parts of her body. The Dream Maker was helping her regain her sexual life, her body life, her life as a woman. It is not easy to live from your body when you have been taught all of your life to "use your head." Lita was trying. Her sex life became intense because she was finally allowing herself to feel her entire body instead of just her genitals. She wanted more; she was no longer satisfied with tender spots—she wanted tenderness.

All of her wanting found direction. She had a dream which would be the turning point for her, a dream she would never forget.

*I dreamt that I was lying in bed and I had four different emotional states. Each one was incredibly powerful. There was one that was too strong for me. When I would start to have it I would back off because I knew I would die. I knew I wanted it, but I didn't know what to do or what was necessary to have it. And then I was in the feeling state again. I got so scared of it I thought I would die. I began crying in the dream; I knew I was dying. Each time I died, I was changed. I could feel my body changing. I knew I wanted it; I wanted my changes. I was crying and knowing. I knew I had found the fourth state.*

The Dream Maker is a guide to becoming a complete person. Lita had finally found what she was missing, what would help her complete her feeling: she had entered into Dream Maker Awareness.

# 7
# "What's So Different and What's So New?"

In the three years since our first encounters with the Dream Maker, we had changed and we had passed on the changes to many of the people around us. In some ways even the city of Los Angeles was a little different; all of our therapists and patients live and work in the city and when they meet people from outside the Center the "outsiders" sometimes notice there is "something different" about them. What is different is that the Center people understand the inner world of dreams and feelings as almost no one else does.

That "something different" about our tribe of people left us with a problem: How could we let other people know about our way of life and how could other people in other places benefit by the Dream Maker Approach? As usual we found the answer to this problem in the dreams of a person from the group.

## Riggs—An Intellectual Solution

Riggs first tried to solve the problem of teaching people outside the therapy about the dream discoveries made inside the therapy by thinking it through. He read about other communities and other therapies and other dream practices and tried to compare their approaches with the Dream Maker Approach. Eventually he wrote a short training paper to teach the other therapists about what he had learned. In the following three paragraphs from this paper you will see what he knew—and what he didn't know.

✦ Psychoanalysts occasionally come across the kinds of dreams we are talking about. Good Gestalt therapists sometimes work with dreams in many of the ways that we do. Certainly Jungian therapists have traversed many Dream Maker regions. And there are other therapies and therapists who have crossed into the Dream Maker Awareness or noticed Breakthru Dreams or the Dream Maker Tradition and perhaps even the Dream Maker Processes. But there was something totally different and completely new about what happened to us. *There was a coming together of three components—therapy, community and dreams—that had never quite happened before, anywhere or anytime.*

There are many good therapies around and a few communities around and a lot of people who work with dreams. But finding each separately is like discovering different parts of an airplane—some people find the motor and say, "This is it," others find the body and say, "This is it," and still others find the inside controls and say, "This is it." No one piece makes the airplane. Here the analogy ends because the purpose of a discovery is not just to find a vehicle, but to use it. In the long run how much time do you really want to spend in an airplane on the ground? What we found was a way to let the three components—therapy, community, and dreams—work together to take us somewhere.

In a community of therapists working together, each can show the others a different direction of life, and something new and exciting comes from each new journey.

What Riggs had taught us was that *we* were the important elements. So often when you discover something new or rediscover something old you forget the blood, sweat, and human tears that go into the discovery. He wouldn't let us forget ourselves. But helping us remember didn't often help him remember. When we would talk Riggs would say: "Dominic taught us through his dreams that there was a new reality, something more. Werner taught us about facing our fears and supporting our community.

Lee taught us about insanity, how to go through and survive. Joe taught us how to 'go easy.' Jerry showed us what thoughts can do. Steve showed us the influence of our past experiences. Lita taught us about our bodies. But what the hell have I done?"

Everyone would try and tell him how important he was to everything that had happened but deep inside he felt left out. Everyone else was an expert in particular ways of understanding dreams and he was more of a jack-of-all-trades with dreams. He knew everything but nothing about his own particular way of dreaming. We all knew that it was only a matter of time—and we did what we had learned: we waited. The Dream Maker had shown us about our pasts and our present and now we were almost ready to witness our future.

It was late October. The Center was very busy . . . with new plans and programs. Riggs was trying to understand how to develop them, but no matter how hard he tried he couldn't seem to make sense of it all.

October in Los Angeles is exciting. Often the Santa Ana winds blow at thirty or forty miles an hour and the city is clear and beautiful. Santa Anas had been blowing for two days. Riggs had worked hard and was now sleeping. His two large dogs, Trucker and Heidi, were sleeping—Trucker at the foot of his bed and Heidi in the living room on the couch. (Sometimes it's hard to tell if he watches over them or they watch over him.) They did not hear this strange man enter the house. He was quiet and knew which room to go to; the Dream Maker had been there before. Without waking Riggs or his wife, Konni, he took Riggs to a dream mountaintop and woke him within his sleep:

*I am on a very high mountaintop via a helicopter ride with Konni. As I sit there I can see an entire island. I am amazed that I can see so far. I can see its makeup. Places where waves break over the reefs. There is not only an island, but an entire island chain. And I can see it all. I was seeing entire episodes of my life. Feeling*

*that things were changing and that I could feel myself moving into*
*a new area of my life. It was as if I was at a vantage point.*

Riggs did not really wake, nor did the dogs stir. Everything was the same the next morning except Riggs. He woke
up happy, kissing Konni's legs and arms. She woke up happy
with all the attention.

It was Thursday. The therapists would be having the dream
group in an hour. Riggs and Konni got up and had coffee
together. She knew something good had happened to him but
she couldn't guess. "What's happening, baby?"

"I had a great dream last night. I have no idea what it
means but I feel great."

They talked and visited but mostly just sat and enjoyed
each other's company. The hour passed quickly and Riggs left
for the dream group. All the therapists loved these groups. It
was a real addition to the therapy. There was always something
very meaningful about learning from each other's dreams.

Dominic asked Riggs what he had dreamt. As he told the
dream he felt the same wave of gladness. Everyone talked about
it.

Usually the group worked with each person's dream, having him express more, make it clearer, feel more, etc. But with
Riggs, Joe had something different in mind.

"Riggs, I don't want you to do anything more with this
dream; I want you to live with it and wait. I think it is just the
first dream of many, a prospective dream; you need to learn to
live with that expanded view of life."

When the meeting was over they left in twos and threes
talking about their dreams. Riggs and Joe went to lunch
together. "You know, Joe, I feel I am losing that good feeling I
had when I woke up."

"That's because you try to do more than you are ready for."

"But if the dream is a prospective dream, what is it telling
me about?"

"Riggs, you should know by now that you can never make your dreams tell you something before you are ready to learn it. Let yourself relax and enjoy the feeling of the dream. It is important to try and live that way for a while."

For ten years these two had worked together and had been friends. They had been through some of the worst times friends could have. They knew each other as do men who know their deepest waking and dream secrets; they knew each other's craziness—and power. As they drank their wine Joe said, "Riggs, I don't want you to work so hard. Just enjoy what your dreams are giving you. I don't think you have really learned to accept and enjoy how much you've changed."

After lunch they went to the YMCA to run off some of that food. Basketball was a great love of their lives. Other therapists and patients were there, and they all played with *feeling;* they cared about each other more than they did the game. Many of the other people at the "Y" would stop and watch these grown men laughing and yelling and playing.

Riggs went home tired; it had been a full day. He knew a lot, but he did not know what the Dream Maker had in store for this night.

Trucker stirred and sat up but nothing bad was happening because tonight the Dream Maker would teach Riggs more about connecting all the parts of the dream puzzle. Riggs would learn that it was the person and not the dream. As he slept he dreamt.

The first dream came early in the night. It was a weave of color and sensation and meaning. It was the completion of the dream he had had the night before.

*I can see myself sleeping. Konni and I are in the bed sleeping very close to each other. I realize that I am watching myself. I don't like that. I am then in bed. I feel very sad and happy. Both feelings were incredibly strong. The more I could feel, the stronger these colors all around me became. It was as if I had these rainbow colors—each different color connecting me to a part of my life. One color*

*like a rainbow led to my past and I understood and felt how it af-*
*fected me; and another color, a soft rose pink, connected to my*
*present and how wonderful it felt to be with Konni and my friends;*
*and another color lead to my future. They were all connected and*
*coming from my body. I felt relaxed down to the molecules in my*
*body. I was close and connected with everything that had hap-*
*pened, was happening, and would happen in my life. The connec-*
*tion was this wonderful happy-sad feeling in my body.*

The dream spun Riggs into a deeper and more relaxed
state. There were more dreams that night, but that is the one he
remembered. When Riggs woke up he was clear; his eyes were
alive.

After seeing his morning patient, Riggs continued to talk
with Joe. "Joe, I found the first answer to the questions I have
been troubled with; I am sure the other questions will be answered. I know from last night that I already have the answers
to my life; I just have to feel myself."

The Dream Maker did not come again with a Breakthru
Dream for over four months. Riggs would need that time to in-
tegrate and live from his understanding of how his past, present,
and future were connected—and he did that. He was awake;
nothing could shake him from what he knew.

Joe would often talk to some of the other staff about it.
Riggs had found his place among the community of dreamers.
There was no leader—each of us fit together to create a new
shaman, a new kind of leader, the group as leader.

As we worked together we tried to devise programs that
would allow more and more people to find out about what we
had discovered. Riggs rejected many ideas because he was afraid
they would dilute our work. But more than anything he wanted
to know that it would be a good thing. He was working very
hard, trying to understand what we needed to do. The work was
interrupted as the Dream Maker returned to give Riggs the
extra insight he needed. This time there was no mountain, only
sand and searching.

*Joe and I are looking for a place for the Center. We are taken by a guide to the edge of the desert. It is vast. I am afraid. There is life there—but the desert life. We realize we must find a place to live which has its own source of water. I am afraid.*

*As we enter the desert without the guide, it is as if we are not separate from it. We live there, have lived there, and are part of it. A large cobra stands in front of us. He seems eighteen feet tall. We—I—crush him. I think of a motto for the Center ("The truth will out")—it goes through two distinct stages: the first is a foot stepping on a cobra and the truth coming out of its mouth; the second is just the words.*

*Then Joe and I are in white desert robes. As we are walking, a band of horsemen appear and are trying to catch us. Joe wants to run. I say, "Drop into the sand and blend with the desert." The horsemen ride over us. Except one man on a smart horse stops. He puts his finger over our breathing straws. I leap out of the sand and like a whirlwind mark him with my breathing straw. I don't have to hurt him. We are free to continue.*

*Then I see a beautiful small lemon tree covered with succulent and beautiful fruit. They are the most beautiful I have ever seen. I see another and another. An entire orchard growing from the sand. It is as if it is life itself.*

*I wake up feeling and saying and realizing I am alive—even in the face of death and dying, I am alive. "I can live, I can do. I am alive. I am alive."*

Joe and Riggs were talking over their morning coffee. Riggs said, "All we have to do is tell people the truth; let them know what we have to offer them. I'm sure that the new programs will come out of the truth that we have to say."

It would have been obvious what was happening if we could have turned around and looked at it historically. The therapy and the community had prepared each individual to have Breakthru Dreams which enabled their strengths to become even clearer. The questions of how to change the therapy, how to change the roles of the therapists and patients were being answered. But that is all content—the process of the therapy, the community, and dreams all coming together was really the major discovery. We had discovered the process of transformation. The Breakthru Dream was becoming a part of the whole process.

A single dream was no longer that important. Finally, after three years' experiences, all the parts were beginning to fit together and we were first beginning to understand them.

This discovery was the beginning and the end—the beginning of a new era and the end of an old. We didn't know it then but we were witnessing the end of the era of psychotherapy. We had taken the next step. We were not doing the therapy—we were living it.

Riggs spent almost four months working with the staff devising new programs. They had finally been able to create programs in which "the truth would out" but not overwhelm. It was so much easier to show people how to pay attention to their dreams than to their deepest feelings. Everyone seemed to want to know about dreams. Riggs was happier but still not satisfied.

It was about this time that The Center Foundation purchased the ranch, a place where the staff would go each summer to renew themselves and do special programs. They would go and work the cattle and the gardens and create and evaluate programs.

One of the things they devised was a Dream Retreat in which people could get to know themselves better through playing and working and slowly learning to talk about their dreams. Without knowing it Riggs and the staff had found the answer to many of their questions. As a person was ready to move from one level of feeling and dreaming to another, he could change his level of involvement. But there was a key—a key that had yet to be fully recognized.

It happened just after the ranch had seen the last group of people leave. The only ones left were the staff. It was time to bring all the summer's firewood closer to the main house. Riggs was tired from working, but it was a good, hard-work tired, not the tiredness that comes from boredom and monotony.

The windows were open and the sweet clean smell of the pines and the oaks drifted through the window. Riggs and Konni were sleeping soundly. The Dream Maker was coming. It would be one of his last mysterious visits; there was no longer a need for the strange and mysterious because these people had become the dream people, new kinds of dreamers.

This dream came only as words. All the words of the therapy and the dream programs were floating in Riggs's head, each one nagging at him. The Dream Maker used the words to teach Riggs: "You are the Dream Makers." As the words came into his mind it was as if the world had been lifted from his shoulders. The words, the searching, were no longer important.

He woke about an hour later and the moon was rising— shining brightly. He got out of bed and looked out the window. Everything was all right. For the first time in a long time the night seemed familiar and good. Everything would be all right for a long time.

Konni sat up. "Riggs, are you okay?"

"Yes, I'm fine. I feel like I'm awake, for the first time in my life I'm all awake."

She slipped out of bed and stood near him. They were two—in a community of many.

Now all our beliefs about dreams were fading. They were no longer so mysteriously special. What was special were the lives we were leading, our everyday lives, every day and every night.

# Part Three

# TWENTY-ONE DAYS TO BREAKTHRU DREAMING— HOW TO MAKE YOUR DREAMS WORK FOR YOU (and Not Against You)

# 8
# Learning How to
# Remember Your Dreams

To begin your education there are four points you must fully understand. One, most people's dreams work against them because they do not pay attention to them. Two, the Breakthru Dreams we have written about do not lead to a bigger, better, shinier you; they lead to a different you, a you who is changing—such changes will be both frightening and deeply satisfying. Three, dreams should not be controlled, manipulated, interpreted, or understood from an intellectual place. Your dream life is like your own wilderness refuge. You cannot take all the trappings of civilization into it, if you want to keep it beautiful and fresh. You will, like we did, eventually become a dream expert. You will know your own dreams and know other people's dreams because you will feel them. Four, don't go to bed trying to change your dreams; that makes dreaming hard work. Remember, dreaming is natural; it happens all by itself. You don't have to work hard all night to experience changes. When you go to bed, let go. Let the Dream Maker do the work. Just follow the exercises we are giving you to prepare yourself.

In the beginning of the book we said we were writing both an adventure story and a discovery book. Whether you know it or not you have already made discoveries while reading this text, discoveries that may not yet have surfaced in your experience. They will.

Dreaming and your Dream Maker Awareness are so keen that they use every bit of information to help you change. In a short while you will notice your dream life is changing.

In this book an intellectual concept or teaching is coupled with a feeling or emotional sense. This coupling is called "affective education." Magic—you learn and remember because the feeling associated with the learning is there.

Many times after our lectures and workshops a person will write to us and say, "I had a dream the other night like I never had before." That is the point of our work; we do not want people to merely understand what we are saying but also to experience it through their own dreams.

This new type of learning is easy. But, don't be fooled by the old maxim, "Easy come, easy go." As we teach you through your feelings it actually becomes harder to forget. You will have not only an intellectual memory of the ideas but also a feeling sense for every word.

We like to present what we call *teachings*. Often the teachings will be concepts, but remember, the overall goal is to learn how to work with the feeling level and process of your dreams.

## Remembering Your Dreams

FIRST TEACHING: IT IS IMPORTANT TO REMEMBER YOUR DREAMS. WHEN YOU REMEMBER YOUR DREAMS YOU REMEMBER YOURSELF.

For many people the first teaching seems like the last because they complain that they cannot remember their dreams. We will teach you how to remember your dreams, but the first step is realizing how important your dream life really is. Imagine forgetting or being unable to remember your sex life!

It seems strange, but many people forget their need to have a full life; they are all work, or all play, or all intellect, or all troubles. They live segmented lives, remembering only parts, often whichever part is convenient. But what is convenient is not necessarily what is the "best" or "the most effective" for *their* lives.

Remembering your dreams is like a very fine reweaving of your life; seemingly unrelated parts begin to fit together. Your dreams help you make sense out of all the parts and pieces of your life, making new patterns for you and redoing old patterns. They tell you what is lacking and what is too much.

What follows is a series of steps for remembering your dreams. Each step gets harder. Depending on what you want to learn about yourself, you will determine which steps you want to take to remember your dreams. You might find that you begin remembering your dreams right away after only one or two exercises. Once you find an exercise that works just right for you, then you will be ready to begin your "Twenty-one Days to Breakthru Dreaming."

## DREAM STEPS

1. Keep in mind that you are trying to remember your dreams. Talk about dreams with your friends. Ask them if they remember their dreams, even if you don't remember yours.

2. If you wake up at the same time every morning, set the clock back half an hour. On weekends go in the other direction. Wake up without an alarm, whenever it happens naturally, the later the better.

3. Keep a pad and pen next to your bed and begin writing down how you feel as soon as you wake up in the morning. Write down anything that you think or feel. Don't try to remember dreams; just be aware of how you feel.

4. Another very good way is to buy a timer and attach it to a light. Instead of waking up to a jarring alarm, have the light set to come on 30 to 45 minutes before the time you usually wake up.

5. Record the events of the previous day as if they were a dream. Be very detailed and specific about how you felt and what you thought.

6. Set your light or alarm to go off four and a half hours after you have fallen asleep. When you awaken, begin writing down anything that has been going on. Then reset the alarm for 30 to 45 minutes before your normal waking time.

7. One of the best ways is to set aside a time right after you have gotten up to sit and talk with someone you have a good relationship with about your nighttime experience. You don't even have to remember a dream. Just tell them how you felt when you awoke and what kind of night's sleep you had. Talk a minimum of 10 minutes.

8. Make up a dream that you would like to have had—a dream that tells you about yourself, your past, and what you need to do in the future.

9. Spend 30 minutes at the end of each day talking with someone about the day you have just lived as if it were a dream.

In these first suggestions about remembering your dreams, you do not have to do anything else; your dreams are your feelings. You don't have to understand them, interpret them, work with them, or Dream Maker them. They are your dreams; let them affect you.

For many people who haven't remembered dreams in years, the increased feeling level they get from remembering is disturbing. But for the majority of people this increased feeling is pleasant and exciting.

As you begin to remember more and more of your dreams, just get to know yourself as a dreamer. You will be surprised at how much feeling you've been holding in. As you allow yourself to really have your dreams they will begin to affect your daytime experiences. By remembering your dreams you will begin to alter your awareness. You will be ready to move toward Breakthru Dreaming and Dream Maker Awareness.

# 9
# Becoming a Dream Maker: Week One

In the following twenty-one-day program you will learn an entirely new way of thinking about and experiencing your dreams. We are going to focus on a single method each week to help you become a Dream Maker and begin having Breakthru Dreams. In Week One all we ask you to do is *be aware*. Once you learn to be aware you may begin to think that we meant "Beware!" It won't be easy but stay with it. We will show you how to be aware of your dreams and the Dream Maker. In Week Two we will teach you how to *identify* your Dream Maker processes. When you learn this skill you are learning something you can use for the rest of your life. Finally, in Week Three we are going to teach you to *change* your Dream Maker processes in waking. Remember, we do not want you to try to change your dreams while you are asleep. As your Indian dream brothers and sisters might have chanted:

> Dream, dream with ease
> Let the dream teach you
> To change the day.

There are many ways that you can approach the next three weeks. You can just answer all the questions silently in your head. That means it will only take you about five minutes a day to complete the questions. Or you can spend up to half an hour a day writing out the answers and recording your experiences in detail. Whichever way you choose you will be surprised at how powerful these questions are; they will stay with you during the day.

You will find yourself going over your dreams and the questions just because it feels good. Thinking about the questions, your answers, and your dreams feels good because they are about you; you will be paying attention to yourself.

Remember, there are no right or wrong answers to any of the questions; there are only your answers. Just noticing your answers will change your dreams naturally.

Each of the twenty-one days means a day that you have remembered a dream. To make this program work most effectively do not go from one day's questions to the next day's questions until you have remembered another dream. We could re-title this section "Twenty-One Dreams to Breakthru Dreaming."

But for those of you who do not want to wait for a daily dream we have devised the "quickie plan." If you wake up in the morning without a dream, write down in your dream notebook (which you should keep next to your bed) how you feel and any thoughts you may have. Then, *make up a dream* from what you have written down. Then answer each day's questions for your made-up dream.

During Week One we are going to teach you to be aware of the four Dream Maker processes. They are *Role* (how you act and move), *Expression* (how you talk and let your feelings out), *Feeling* (what you experience in the dream or about the dream), and *Clarity* (how clear and easy to follow the dream story is and how aware you are in the dream).

In the exercises that follow we will ask you to be aware of these processes in your dreams, in your waking experiences, and in your body. During Week One we are not trying to make very detailed connections between these three parts of your life. Instead we are teaching you to become aware that many of the same processes which happen to you during the day are also at work in your dreams.

# Day One—Role

Write down your dream and then answer these questions:

## DREAM QUESTIONS
1. Are you as the dreamer active or passive in this dream?
2. Do you have the starring role in this dream or a secondary part?
3. Do you like the way you are in this dream?
4. Are you participating in this dream or just observing?
5. What is the main form of activity in the dream?
6. List all the different roles (ways of doing things, or talking, or moving, or acting) in this dream. Choose the one you like the most.

## WAKING QUESTIONS
1. Is your role in this dream similar to your role in waking?
2. Think about your role in sex, play, work, and relationships.

## BODY QUESTIONS
1. Are you aware of the details of your own body movements in the dream? In waking? For example, are you aware of the body sensations of running, hitting, moving your arms, walking, or whatever you were doing?

# Day Two—Expression

When we talk about Expression at the simplest level we mean noise. Think about your dreams without any pictures or people at all, just sounds. Think about trying to identify your dream by sounds or noise.

## DREAM QUESTIONS
1. How expressive are you in this dream?
2. What is your main form of expression?

3. Is your expression the main expression in the dream? Or are other forms of expression more dominant?
4. List all the kinds of expression in the dream, the most dominant expressions first.
    a. Most Dominant Expression _____
    b. Next Strongest Expression _____
    c. Third Strongest Expression _____

## WAKING QUESTIONS
1. Is this the same style of expression that you use in waking?
2. Do you like the way you are expressing in this dream? In waking?
3. What would you think about yourself if other people saw you expressing the same way in waking as you do in this dream?
4. Are there more things you would like to express in the dream but hold in for different reasons? In waking? List them.

## BODY QUESTIONS
1. What parts of your body are you aware of as you express in the dream?
2. What parts of your body are you unaware of in this dream?
3. What parts of your body seem restricted or missing?

## DREAM MAKER QUESTION
Do you believe you have the potential to express more than you do in this dream?

# Day Three—Feeling

Day Three begins to order the questions of Days One and Two so they make more sense. As you try to understand what we mean by feeling, think about the entire dream without words or movement or any picture at all—just imagine that the dream is a body feeling; like being pinched—you feel it. Often people dream dreams that have feeling in them, but the dreamer doesn't feel anything. When we discuss feeling, we mean both how you felt as the dreamer and how the dream feels to you overall. We are going to teach you to be aware of these possibilities.

## DREAM QUESTIONS

1. What is your feeling level in this dream?
2. What is the overall feeling in this dream?
3. What feelings do you as the dreamer experience in the dream?
4. List all the different feelings in this dream, putting the most dominant first:
   a. _____
   b. _____
   c. _____

## WAKING QUESTIONS

1. Think about all the feelings you had today. Which was the strongest? The weakest?
2. List the feelings you normally do *not* have.
   a. _____
   b. _____
   c. _____
3. What feelings do you have about yourself? (Do you like yourself? Do you like some things and dislike others?)

## BODY QUESTIONS

1. Here is a list of all the parts of your body. Rate how much you feel in each part. 1 (a little), 2 (an average), 3 (a lot)

| | | | |
|---|---|---|---|
| head_____ | shoulders_____ | chest_____ | pelvic_____ |
| eyes_____ | arms_____ | stomach_____ | genitals_____ |
| jaw_____ | hands_____ | back_____ | buttocks_____ |
| | fingers_____ | lower back_____ | thighs_____ |
| | | | calves_____ |
| | | | feet_____ |
| | | | toes_____ |

# Day Four—Clarity

Clarity is the fourth of the Dream Maker processes and ties all four processes together. What you will find is that as you identify each process in your dreams each process will become stronger. You will begin to notice connections between processes—e.g., that when you are passive in a dream you usually are also unclear. We will teach you more about those connections later. For the moment, keep in mind that the Dream Maker Approach gives you a new way of thinking which eliminates good and bad. Now you can understand your dreams as a dynamic process.

## DREAM QUESTIONS

1. How clear is this dream?
   a. How vivid were the colors?
   b. Was it fuzzy? Or was it a clear dream picture?
   c. Did you understand everything that happened in your dream when you woke up?
   d. Did the dream make sense as it happened?
2. How clear were you as the dreamer? Did you know the details of what was happening in this dream as you were dreaming? For example, did you know why you were doing things and what you were doing?
3. Which character in the dream seemed to understand what was happening the most?
4. List the characters in order of how clear they were:
   a. _____
   b. _____
   c. _____

## WAKING QUESTIONS

1. How clear are you at work? In sex? At play? In your relationships?
2. Do you act on what you know? Or do you silently think about things?

3. Do things just seem to happen to you? Or do you know the cause and effect of what is going on in your life?
4. Are other people in your life clearer than you are?
5. Which character in this book was the clearest?

**BODY QUESTIONS**
1. While you were dreaming, did you clearly see your body in the dream? What parts were missing?

You have just learned how to look at dreams in a new way. A really good thing for you to do is to teach someone else what you have just learned. Talk to someone at work about dreams. You'll see that they are like you were before you started reading these chapters; they will want to know what everything means and why. For now, teach them the four basic processes. Remember, you do not have to be a dream expert; we are the teachers and you are the students. You can also be a teacher. Enjoy both.

# Day Five—Combining the Four Processes

**DREAM QUESTIONS**
1. Think about the four Dream Maker processes (Role, Expression, Feeling, and Clarity) that you have just learned and ask yourself the following questions:
    a. How do they seem to interact?
    b. Which one seems the most important?
    c. Do you have mental blocks against some and not others?
2. Do you notice in your dreams that sometimes one of these processes is stronger than the rest?

**WAKING QUESTIONS**
1. List three situations in which you can remember being aware of all four of these components.

2. Name one person whom you have met who seemed to have all of these qualities strongly developed.
3. For each process, name one person who you think has that particular process strongly developed.

# Day Six

Today, do not work with the dreams you remember. Instead: Make up a dream-story which includes sex, work, play, and relationships in which you are aware of the four Dream Maker processes: Role, Clarity, Feeling, and Expression.

# Day Seven

This is a Dream Maker day. Make up an exercise that you think would help you become a Dream Maker. Every other day you have followed our exercises. Today, be inventive and make up your own. It can be anything, the content of the exercise is less important than doing it because it is the doing that really helps you *pay* attention to your dreams. (We're serious when we say the exercise can be *anything*. If you want you could eat banana ice cream while standing on your head and that would be a good Dream Maker exercise. You'd never forget it!)

# The End of Week One

Before we begin Week Two, take a look back and review what you have learned. The four Dream Maker processes are important not only in your dreams but also in all aspects of your waking life. For example, people often try to understand why they are unhappy with their sex lives, when it would actually be a lot simpler for them to understand that they are being less expressive throughout their lives than they want to be. Think about how these four processes are involved in *every* aspect of your life.

Use the next several teachings we present to bring together your own experiences of the first week.

SECOND TEACHING: YOUR DREAMS AND FEELINGS CAN WORK FOR YOU OR AGAINST YOU.

## Making Dreams Work for You

In this book we have tried to teach you that your dreams and all the feelings that are present in dreams are very important. Of course we are not the first psychologists to emphasize the importance of dreams. The main school of thought about dreams is the psychoanalytic "what" school. This school says that dreams are important because of what they hide. Dream interpretation is like hide and seek. There are also many "sub-what" schools, each one encouraging people to find a particular kind of interpretation which comes from asking, "What—what does this part of the dream mean and what does that mean?"

While "what" will always remain an important question, it must be shifted to a secondary position. The first line of questions begins with "how." In switching to "how" questions we can begin to look at dreams from the functional/dynamic viewpoint. This way of looking at dreams replaces understanding the dream with observing how the dream functions. The Dream Maker Approach generates a new series of functional questions you can use to help yourself work with your own dreams.

A dreamer can gain immediate insight into his own dream processes, without trying to decipher his dream symbols. When a dreamer begins to see, understand, and experience his own dream dynamics or processes, he is moving his dream world from the mysterious and symbolic to the real and functional, from the clinical and interpretive to the personal.

What is so different about this functional/dynamic or Dream Maker Approach is that most modern-day research and clinical work is concerned with the interpretation of content. The difficulty we had in accepting the interpretive/content approach was that it did not lead to anything else except more interpretation. That consequence dictates that the normal dreamer will continue waking up in the morning needing to interpret his dream or have his dream interpreted by someone else. We believe that if the Interpretive Orientation were correct it would lead to dreams that did not need interpretation, just as the Dream Maker Approach leads to Breakthru Dreams. We have simplified understanding the dream to the same dynamic level as understanding how an engine works or how the heart functions. If all the parts work together effectively then the dream is working for the dreamer.

### THIRD TEACHING: DREAMS ARE FEELINGS.

This simple little teaching will take you years to fully understand. In our more technical theory we say dreams are pictures of feelings. When we take time to really understand this it becomes very involved. But this third teaching will help you make the shift from dreams working against you to dreams working for you; it is like acquiring a bank account you never knew you had. Imagine going to the bank and asking for your life savings and being told, "Something happened to your money, we can't remember what." You'd be upset and certainly try to find out what happened. But how often have you awakened from a night's sleep and said, "I dreamt something last night, but I just can't remember what."? That something that happened adds up to one-third of your life. And it is the one-third of your life where your feelings are uninterrupted by your daily routine duties and distractions.

### FOURTH TEACHING: DREAMS ARE A COMPLETION PROCESS.

Dreams are attempts to complete feelings left incomplete from the preceding day or from the past. Besides trying to complete specific feelings, dreams are trying to complete the process of feeling. That means the dream is trying to shift or change or transform your way of feeling that has been carried over from childhood. Any single dream is working for the dreamer when it completes the feelings left incomplete from the previous day. And it becomes transformative when it shifts the dreamer from past processes to new and transformative processes.

FIFTH TEACHING: DREAMS ARE A PICTURING PROCESS.

Dreams picture for us what life is really like. What confuses many people is that they believe only a very crazy person would have crazy dreams. We aren't talking about very crazy people; we are talking about normally crazy people.

Normal neurotics (almost everyone) do things in waking which are not direct—i.e., most people live symbolic lives. The symbolism of their waking life goes unnoticed because everyone else is doing the same—*except* at night. Then normal people have dreams which picture them as they really are—symbolic and confused.

What we teach in this book is how to have Dream Maker dreams. The people we wrote about changed their daytime feelings and their dreams changed in parallel, becoming less and less symbolic and working for them.

Here are some additional exercises which parallel the four processes we have presented. All of these exercises help you help your Dream Maker. Try these:

*Step One: Make a list of daytime situations in which you do not complete your feelings—situations in which you are aware that you don't say, feel, or express all that is in you.*

What we are trying to teach is that dreams attempt to complete feelings. To understand dreams, it is often easier to look at waking experiences first. The parallel relationship between dreams and waking is simple. When you continue to have feelings each day that do not get expressed or felt, your dreams continue to be symbolic. A symbolic dream does not complete feelings, actions, or expressions. That means it is not working effectively for you.

A dream works for you when it completes. Waking, then,

can also work for you by completing feeling through expression and action. When you have *both* your waking life working for you *and* your dream life working, then you are ready to learn from the pictures in your dreams what you need to do next.

*Step Two: With the dreams that you have remembered so far, just look at the picture of you that your dream is showing. Simply ask yourself, "Is this the way I would like to live the rest of my life?"*

When you are aware of your dream dynamics, and of how those dynamics operate in waking, and of the pictures your dreams are showing you, then you are ready for a closer look at the processes which influence your dreams and feelings.

# 10
# Becoming a Dream Maker: Week Two

Unlike many "how-tos" that promise miraculous results for no work, our "how-tos" are different. The difference between miracle therapy and this dynamic "how-to" is tremendous as you will see later on. Even though we have given you many exercises in Week One, we want now to give you more.

But this week we are going to change our emphasis—we will move from simple awareness to active identifying. During Week Two we want you to identify your Dream Maker processes in detail day by day. We are going to take the four Dream Maker processes that you became aware of in Week One and extend your knowledge of how they function. In Week Two we will graph each of the four processes by themselves and then all together. What we want you to do is to identify each process by itself and then slowly we will help you use all of them at once.

## Day Eight—Graphing Your Role

Write down your dream and then answer the questions and use the graph.

**DREAM QUESTIONS**

1. Remember, by role we mean how physically active you are in your dreams, how much you move your body—arms, legs, hands, etc.
2. Now we want you to graph or plot how active you are in your

dreams. Generally, taking all of your dreams into consideration, how active are you in your dreams?

1＿＿＿No role  (You have no role in the dream.)

2＿＿＿Passive  (You are only a part of the dream. Your role is that of someone who is present but uninvolved and unresponsive.)

3＿＿＿Slightly active  (There is some response by you to dream events, but for the most part your role does not change the outcome of the dream.)

4＿＿＿Active  (Your activity is obvious in the dream. Your role in response to events is complete.)

5＿✓＿Very active (Your activity dominates the dream.)

3.  Graph your role.

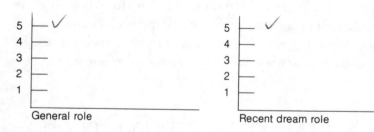

General role                    Recent dream role

4.  Now do the same graphing for your most recent dream.

## PAST QUESTIONS

1.  Using the 1 to 5 ratings from above, write down the number for your waking role that best describes the way you were

during the following periods of your life: 1 year to 5 years; 6 to 12; 13 to 16; 17 to 21; 22 to 25; 26 to 35; 36 to 45; 46 to 55; 56 to 65 +.

2. Graph your role for each period of your life.

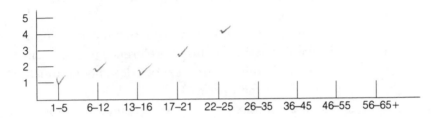

## WAKING QUESTIONS

1. Now look at the last graph. Notice if your role has changed over the years. Think about what has happened to you, how you have changed.
2. Think about how your parents, your friends, and your culture have determined your role.
3. Are you satisfied with your role in waking?
4. What are three beliefs you have about how you should be in waking?

## DREAM MAKER QUESTION

What special strengths do you have that you don't use?

# Day Nine—Graphing Your Expression

**DREAM QUESTIONS**

1. Decide how expressive you are generally in your dreams.

   1_____No expression   (No outward expression of any type of feeling or thought by you.)

   2_____Slight   (Some expression, but it is relegated to a minor feature.)

   3_____Moderate   (Definite but not striking expression.)

   4_____Strong   (Expression takes preference over all your other activities, but does not dominate the dreams.)

   5_____Intense   (Prolonged and complete expression of feeling. Expression dominates dreams, even in the face of obstacles.)

2. Graph your expression.

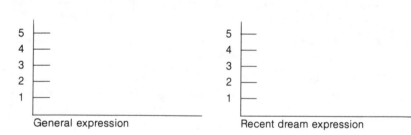

General expression                    Recent dream expression

3. Now follow the same graphing for your most recent dream.

**PAST QUESTIONS**

1. Rate your expression—write down the number for your expression that best describes the way you were during the

following periods of your life: 1 year to 5 years; 6 to 12; 13 to 16; 17 to 21; 22 to 25; 26 to 35; 36 to 45; 46 to 55; 56 to 65+.

2. Graph your expression for each period of your life.

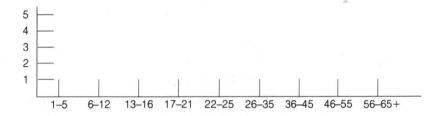

## WAKING QUESTIONS

1. Notice if your expression has changed over the years. Think about what happened to you, how you have changed.
2. Think about how your parents, your friends, and your culture have determined your expression.
3. Are you satisfied with your expression in waking?
4. List what types of expression were okay as you were growing up and what kinds were frowned upon.

| *Okay* | *Frowned Upon* |
|--------|----------------|
| 1.     | 1.             |
| 2.     | 2.             |
| 3.     | 3.             |
| 4.     | 4.             |

## DREAM MAKER QUESTION

Do you notice when other people really want to express more but hold back? What do you think when you see them do it?

# Day Ten–Graphing Your Feeling Level

## DREAM QUESTIONS

1. Decide how much feeling you generally have in your dreams.

   1 _____ No feeling  (Your dreams are about things or events that remain neutral.)

   2 _____ Slight  (Your dream evokes some feeling, but the feeling is vague and in the background.)

   3 _____ Moderate  (Your dreams contain some feeling that is not vague, but the feeling does not dominate or even greatly influence your dreams.)

   4 _____ Strong  (Your dreams contain definite feeling, more than is usually evident in normal waking life; but the feeling does not dominate.)

   5 _____ Intense  (The feeling overrides all else in the dream. You are aware that you are feeling and allow it to fully occur.)

2. Graph your general dream feeling level.

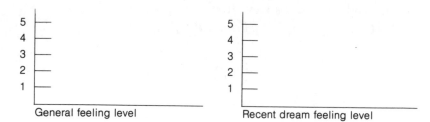

General feeling level          Recent dream feeling level

3. Now graph your feeling level in your most recent dream.

## PAST QUESTIONS

1. Rate your feeling—write down the number for your feeling level that best describes the way you were during the following periods of your life: 1 year to 5 years; 6 to 12; 13 to 16; 17 to 21; 22 to 25; 26 to 35; 36 to 45; 46 to 55; 56 to 65+.
2. Graph your feeling level for each period of your life.

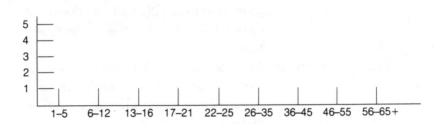

## WAKING QUESTIONS

1. Notice if your feeling level has changed over the years. Think about what happened to you, how you have changed.
2. Think about how your parents, your friends, and your culture have determined your feeling level.
3. Are you satisfied with your feeling level in waking?
4. What kinds of feelings were okay for you as a child?
    1.
    2.
    3.
5. What kinds of feelings were not tolerated?
    1.
    2.
    3.

# Day Eleven—Graphing Your Clarity

**DREAM QUESTIONS**

1. Decide how much general clarity you have in your dreams.

   1 _____ Completely confused  (Your dream pictures are incoherent. Events and feelings have no relationship.)

   2 _____ Unclear and indirect  (There is much distortion in your dreams, although it does not completely obscure the dream pictures.)

   3 _____ Somewhat clear and direct  (You have a general idea of what is going on in the dreams, even though some elements may be distorted.)

   4 _____ Clear and direct  (Your pictures are clear and direct but not complete.)

   5 _____ Completely clear and direct  (Your feelings and actions are totally clear and direct. There is no distortion.)

2. Graph your general clarity.

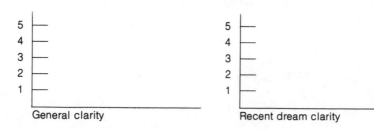

General clarity                    Recent dream clarity

3. Now graph the clarity in your most recent dream.

## PAST QUESTIONS

1. Rate your clarity—write down the number for your clarity that best describes the way you were during the following periods of your life: 1 year to 5 years; 6 to 12; 13 to 16; 17 to 21; 22 to 25; 26 to 35; 36 to 45; 46 to 55; 56 to 65+.
2. Graph your clarity for each period of your life.

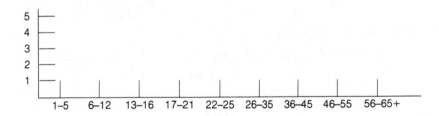

## WAKING QUESTIONS

1. Notice if your clarity has changed over the years. Think about what happened to you, how you have changed.
2. Think about how your parents, your friends, and your culture have determined your level of clarity.
3. Are you satisfied with your clarity in waking?

## DREAM MAKER QUESTION

What would you be like if you attained or experienced Satori or a Breakthru experience?

Days Seven, Eight, Nine, and Ten are very important days. Whether or not you know it, we have asked you to think about things that most people try to avoid. Often people blame themselves for being a certain way without ever realizing that they were forced to be that way as they grew up and that now, if they could understand their Dream Maker processes, they could change.

Before you go to Days Twelve, Thirteen, and Fourteen, go back over your last four days and take a look at how your life has developed.

Then go on.

# Day Twelve

## DREAM QUESTIONS

1. Graph today's dream and yesterday's waking for all four components. Use X for dream, O for waking.

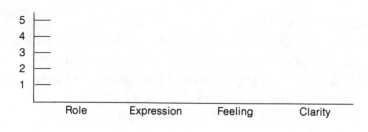

2. Notice which is your greatest strength.
3. Do you depend on it very often?
4. How would you change if you developed other Dream Maker processes and your waking processes?
5. Do you see any parallels between your Dream Maker processes and your waking processes?

Day Twelve is the most sophisticated day of all. In order to do it correctly you need to understand all of the other days. But Day Twelve is also a day of really beginning to understand how each dream works overall. It becomes much simpler to understand dreams when you are able to look at them from the Dream Maker perspective. Now, you can look at any dream and ask the questions that tell you "how the dream is put together." You will begin to notice that your dreams have certain characteristics. Maybe they are low in clarity when you don't express or they are very clear when your role is very active. There are no special combinations; we want you to begin noticing what *your* processes are.

# Day Thirteen

## QUESTIONS
1. Graph a waking experience for all four components.

2. Think about someone you really like.
   a. What are their processes like?
   b. How would they need to change to become more balanced?

# Day Fourteen

## QUESTIONS

1. Graph your dream life and waking life for all four processes. Use an X for the dream and an O for the waking experience.

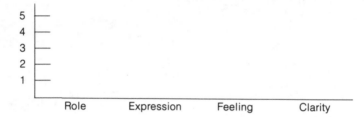

2. Exercise: Allow your strongest Dream Maker Process to become even stronger today. Identify and experience it in waking.

## Week Two—Summary

When these four components are balanced (at some plus one point on the graph) they are all even. Balance gives you a foundation for change.

It becomes easy to understand how some people complain of "being in their heads" or "being an intellectual" when their clarity is higher than the rest of the components. Other people are hysterical; all they do is express. Anything that happens is just another excuse for them to respond with another superficial expression. Other people are called "moody" when they have only a strong feeling score. Others are "hyperactive" when their strongest score is role. When these four components are balanced the dreamer feels good.

Even in a symbolic dream, if it has balanced components, the dreamer can know and feel his dreams working for him. On the other hand, when any single component is way out of line, the person is out of balance. We will not explain this further now because it becomes increasingly complex. But in workshops and therapy we work with every person to help him tune or balance his individual processes. Here are some things you can understand:

a) These dynamic processes *determine* how you are in the pictures in your dreams.

b) Most people try to change the picture through understanding, when in fact changing the processes changes the picture through action.

What begins to emerge from these graphs is a picture of your dreaming and waking dynamics, what your strengths and weaknesses are. You do not have to do anything about them; for now just identify them. Your dreams are trying to show you in what ways you are imbalanced. Once you know of the imbalance then you naturally begin to correct or balance yourself.

When all the dynamics balance, then you begin having Dream Maker experiences. Your dreams become more intense. Because our therapy and our dream findings are so interrelated we made connections between them. In our therapy we work with a person's past, present, and future.

TEACHING SIX: YOUR DREAMS TELL YOU ABOUT YOUR PAST, PRESENT, AND FUTURE.

Our concept of dreams as dynamic pictures of feelings allows us to say that dreams tell a person about his past, present, and future. Feelings are the personal weave and connection between a person's past (what happened to his feelings as a child and how he learned to express his feelings), present (what is happening to his feelings as an adult, how he is affected by other people and situations, and how he is affecting the world around him), and his future (what is his potential to feel).

When a person leads a very narrow existence, then as he grows older his options to change become less and less. This means his dreams will show him how little of a future his feelings really have. But as a person begins to feel more and open himself up more, then he is literally creating his future.

As we have shown earlier, dreams can help a person directly experience what it was like for him or her as a child. This experience then shows someone how he continues to act in a way as an adult which is really appropriate only for what happened to him as a child.

## THREE EXTRA EXERCISES

*Past:* In any of your dreams, identify and list the ways in the dream that you felt, acted, and thought that were like the way you were as a child.

*Present:* Try to identify in your most recent dream a single way of expressing, feeling, acting, or understanding that is completely yours as an adult.

*Future:* See how you could have changed or completed your most recent dream: 1) How could you have changed your expression (the quality, intensity, variety)? 2) How could you have changed your clarity? 3) How could you have changed the expressions you used in the dream? 4) How could you have changed the actions you used in the dream? 5) How would changing any of these affect the overall outcome of the dream?

Remember, all of the exercises we have given you are doorways to new discoveries about your dreams. You don't have to do more with them; they will lead you to more change.

Once you become expert at answering these questions clearly then you will understand how dreams can really help you experience your past, present, and future. The dreams in and of themselves can begin to affect your waking life. When a person repeatedly takes the steps we have outlined, his dreams will slowly stop working against him.

Literally, most people wake up from their dreams with a minus; they spend the day trying to recover from that minus awakening. When a person is able to work with dreams in the simple ways we have just outlined, he can quickly change a symbolic censored dream into a plus. His dreams begin working for him. When the cycle of minus awakening is broken, the dreamer is closer to having a Breakthru Dream which will start him on his plus awakening and on to Dream Maker Awareness.

What is the Breakthru Dream and the Dream Maker Awareness that comes with it? When a person pays attention to his dreams then it becomes possible for him to attain a new level of awareness. What this awareness is *exactly* is a new reference point. It is like finding a place to live within yourself. And this place feels different and literally gives you a new address. You no longer return to your old ways of dreaming and acting.

Surprisingly, what is difficult about having a Breakthru Dream and attaining Dream Maker Awareness is realizing that it is not something foreign to you. It is something you have had since childhood, but lost. Now, as you become a Dream Maker, you rediscover what you had as a child, a clear and vivid awareness in waking that allows you to dream dreams which give you an internal direction for your life.

There is a connection between waking and dreaming, and the past and the present, and the connection becomes clear when you identify the Dream Maker processes. You have now learned to identify yourself in a new way, using the functional viewpoint. This new method frees you from trying to interpret your own behavior; now you can look at yourself and others with new understanding.

Remember that it is a good idea to try and begin teaching a friend about his Dream Maker processes. This will allow you to test how clearly you understand the dream teachings up to this point.

# II
# Becoming
# a Dream Maker:
# Week Three

Over the last fourteen days you have been learning and trying out new things—all in preparation for Week Three when we will begin teaching you how to *change* your dreams by changing your dynamics. It is an educational process whose real test takes place at night. If you learn the teachings we present, then you will naturally begin including them in your dreams. The easy way to pretest yourself is by trying out the methods in waking.

So far we have given you a giant-sized dose of our theories both intellectually and experientially. However, as you have probably noticed, we have not tried to explain what each exercise means. You will find that as you do the exercises your dreams will naturally and simply change. The changes are more important than explanations of how the changes happen.

In Week Three we are going to shift the emphasis one more time. We have already taught you to be aware and to identify— and now we add *changes*. When we talk about change we are asking you to defy some of your internal limits—to break your waking pictures of yourself. Week Three gets a little scarier because we ask you to begin introducing your Dream Maker to your daytime life.

If you don't try *anything* new in waking, your progress will stop; if you try too much you'll get discouraged. Let yourself try little new steps.

# Day Fifteen–Role

Take your dream and look at your role. Here are some questions to ask yourself:

**DREAM QUESTIONS**
1. Are you satisfied with your role in this dream?
2. What would have to happen in this dream so that you could be totally satisfied with your role in this dream?
3. What is your main role in this dream?
4. How do you keep your role incomplete?
5. What would you have to do to complete it?
6. Does your role in this dream work for you or against you?
7. How would you have to change your role to make this a Breakthru Dream?
8. Rate your role level in this dream. What would it be like if you took it one higher? One lower?
9. List all your fears of what would happen if you raised your role to a Breakthru level.

**WAKING QUESTIONS**
   Try to change your role today. As you notice your role, lessen it a little and then increase it. Try this out all day long.

   Before you go to Day Sixteen—did you really try out some of those new things? If not, at least be aware and identify the processes you used to stop yourself. Did you become less clear? Less active? Less expressive? Did you restrict your feeling level?

# Day Sixteen–Expression

**DREAM QUESTIONS**
1. Are you satisfied with your expression in this dream?

2. What would have to happen in this dream so that you would be totally satisfied with your expression?
3. What is your main expression in this dream?
4. How do you keep your expression incomplete?
5. What would you have to do to complete it?
6. How would you have to change your expression to make this a Breakthru Dream?
7. Does the expression in this dream work for you or against you?
8. Rate your expression level in this dream. What would it be like if you took it one higher? One lower?

## DREAM MAKER QUESTION
What good things would happen if you began to express using your Dream Maker *potential?*

## WAKING QUESTIONS
On Day Sixteen you learned more about expression. Now we want you to combine Days Fifteen and Sixteen and try to match your role and your level of expression all day long. When you are passive let your expression go way down; when you are active let your expression increase.

# Day Seventeen—Feeling

## DREAM QUESTIONS
1. Are you satisfied with your feeling level in this dream?
2. What would have to happen in this dream so that you would be totally satisfied with your feeling level?
3. What is your main feeling in this dream?
4. How do you keep your feeling incomplete?
5. What would you have to do to complete it?
6. How would you have to change your feeling level to make this a Breakthru Dream?

7. Does the feeling in this dream work for you or against you?
8. Rate your feeling level in this dream. What would it be like if you took it one higher? One lower?

## DREAM MAKER QUESTION

What would happen to your body if you had more feeling?

## WAKING QUESTIONS

Remember Day Sixteen's waking experience. Repeat it, but add a third Dream Maker Process. This time try and match your waking feeling with your role and expression. Pretend you are a very fine guitar that needs to be tuned. Be aware all day long how often your role, feeling, and expression go out of tune with each other.

# Day Eighteen–Clarity

## DREAM QUESTIONS

1. Are you satisfied with your clarity in this dream?
2. What would have to happen in this dream so that you would be totally satisfied with your clarity?
3. What are you most clear about in this dream?
4. How do you keep yourself confused?
5. What would you have to do to be completely clear?
6. How would you have to change your clarity to make this a Breakthru Dream?
7. Does the clarity in this dream work for you or against you?
8. Rate your clarity level in this dream. What would it be like if you took it one higher?

## DREAM MAKER QUESTION

What would happen to all your problems if you became very clear?

# Day Nineteen–All the Dynamics

**DREAM QUESTIONS**
1. Rate all four Dream Maker processes for your dream.
2. Imagine redreaming the dream. Increase each one of the four dynamics by one level.
3. Would that increase your satisfaction?
4. Would that change the way you feel about yourself?

**WAKING QUESTIONS**
1. How would it affect your waking life if you changed each one of those four components?
2. What are your fears of what would happen?
3. What good things do you think would happen?
4. What problems would be solved?

**DREAM MAKER QUESTION**

Try to live for three minutes today with more feeling, role, expression, and clarity—all at a matched level.

# Day Twenty–Finding Your Dream Maker Word

## DREAM QUESTIONS

1. List the twenty main words you could use to describe what is happening in your dream. Reduce that to ten, and then to five, then to three, then to two, then to one. That single word is your Dream Maker word. Live from your Dream Maker word all through the day.

1.
2.
3.
4.
5.
6.      1.
7.      2.
8.      3.          1.
9.      4.          2.      1.
10.     5.          3.      2.      1.
11.     6.          4.      3.      2.      1.
12.     7.          5.
13.     8.
14.     9.
15.     10.
16.
17.
18.
19.
20.

# Day Twenty-one—Maintaining the Changes

Your dreams have certainly begun to change already. Here is a series of questions you can use to maintain the change.

1. How did this dream feel to you?
2. How did you like the way you were expressing?
3. How did you like the role you had in this dream?
4. How did you like your clarity in this dream?
5. How did you like your feeling level in this dream?
6. Are you giving equal attention to all four of the Dream Maker components?
7. What is this dream trying to tell you about your waking life?
8. What is this dream trying to tell you about your future?
9. How can you change these processes so that the picture works for you?

This is not a quickie calisthenics program to shape up for the summer, so you do not stop the exercises here. Repeat any exercise as often as you want, and as often as you need it.

By continuing the Dream Maker Approach you can continue to use any dream for yourself instead of against yourself. The functional approach is always the same—be aware, identify, and then balance your Dream Maker processes. Balancing will always lead to a Breakthru. By sharing your dreams with other people you can extend the Dream Maker Tradition into the future. Every Breakthru Dream you experience will lead you farther, by giving you your own direction for that day and time in your life. You do not need to keep getting twenty-second, twenty-third, etc., exercises from us.


We have tried to convey the fact that you have dreams inside of you that you keep losing; we want you to find them, keep them, and use them. We have also tried to show you how your feelings and your dreams are connected, in fact, how they are dynamically interwoven with your past and present.

But past and present are not enough; everyone needs a real future. We are really trying to teach you how to determine your future. If you become an expert at understanding your dream processes and working with them, *you will change your future.* New realms of feeling and dreaming will open to you. That is a big goal—but not too big.

We will certainly write more books in our future and continue to live using our dreams and feelings as allies rather than enemies. We will cry and shout and laugh and dream—and share everything. We want you to do the same.

What is perhaps the most difficult thing we have taught you is that if you do these things you *will* change. Everyone wants change and fears it at the same time.

If we were to give you one more exercise it would be to list all the changes you want to have in your life for the next year. Now, say to yourself, "I am *good* enough to change." It's impossible to change if you try to be just "not-so-bad." You can really change only from a good inner sense of yourself. That is what the Dream Maker brings: the strongest, surest, wisest inner sense you could ask for. By reacquainting you with your Dream Maker and teaching you about the Dream Maker processes we have given you the means to radically change your future. Use them and become a Dream Maker.

# Part Four

# APPLYING THE DISCOVERY— A DREAM MAKER WORKSHOP

# 12
# Who Is
# the Dream Maker?

After a time, we came to firmly trust our discoveries. We knew we could use dreams to help ourselves. We knew we could rely on the Dream Maker Process. But we did not know how transmittable our discovery of the Dream Maker would be. Could other people have Breakthru Dreams without going through our intensive therapy? Could people change from their dreams alone? Could we pass on the Dream Maker Tradition and extend our community? Could a person be taught to use the Dream Maker Process to overcome the Censoring Process? There were still many unanswered questions.

Riggs's guiding dreams had told us we could just teach people by having them live with us. We gradually developed a whole series of programs, ranging from short contact correspondence programs to long range live-in programs. We learned that people who wanted more change would live with us closer and longer, and people who wanted the most would evolve their own Dream Maker communities.

Our first big extension of the Dream Maker Approach occurred with a group of nine French-Canadian psychologists from Montreal. They had read our book *Going Sane* and heard us speak about dreams when we were on an East Coast lecture tour. They contacted us, asking for professional training. We arranged a Community Training Program for them in early 1976 to teach them how they could work together as a group. We injected into this program a big dose of Dream Maker training, and it worked. Within two months the Canadians were dreaming differently and living differently. They took back with them to Canada a new but hardy Dream Maker Tradition.

Next, we began to offer a few one-day workshops to the general public; we wanted to know how individuals would respond to the Dream Maker Approach. It was more difficult for individuals than for groups, but we found out they could do it. We began to give more Dream Maker workshops.

Every Dream Maker workshop is different because we make changes according to the interests and experiences of the participants. The workshop we describe in the next four chapters traces the experiences of two people, Michael and Judy, who attended a Dream Maker workshop in Chicago in 1976.

A young man who is dissatisfied invites in what is frightening. Recently, Michael had been asking himself some questions— "What do I want? Is this the way life is? Is this all there is to life?" Such questions draw the Dream Maker closer.

When Michael was a child, the Dream Maker had come in his night terrors. Michael's parents always told him, "It's just a dream." But now there were no parents, and he was no longer a child. Up those long corridors from Michael's childhood the Dream Maker made his way.

It is 1:30 A.M. Michael is floating deep in sleep. He is dreaming that the Dream Maker is coming. Even in his sleep he is aware that something is wrong, something is terribly wrong. His heart begins to beat faster. His breathing becomes shallow. He feels it nudge him. The Dream Maker is close. Michael tries to regain consciousness. He tries to get out of that sleep. Even in his deepest sleep he is aware of what is happening. It is more than a nightmare. His body feels squeezed. He feels himself being dragged under—deeper into another world. As he spins and swirls in sleep he knows this is not just a nightmare; this will not pass with waking.

What Michael didn't know was that he would no longer

be the same. He would not look the same nor act the same. His relationship with his girl friend Judy would change. His work would change. It would be months before he would fully know what had happened to him.

The Dream Maker is not new for anyone. He has been around in everyone's life since childhood. Each of us knew the Dream Maker all those times when we sat up in bed, crying, knowing something was wrong, but not able to understand it, or say it, or show it. And since we couldn't share our knowing, it became a secret that each of us keeps secured deep inside until we sleep and dream.

The Dream Maker came to Michael and Judy at just this time in their lives because they were ready to share their feelings; they were ready to be vulnerable and share secrets with each other.

By the time Michael was able to wake himself and ease the grip of the Dream Maker, he could not remember exactly what had happened. Something had happened, but he didn't know what. He sat up in bed with a start, his body sweating. He looked around in the darkness. The clock glowed and showed the time—6:30 A.M. His girl friend, Judy, stirred. She slept so peacefully, so soundly, "without a trouble in the world," he thought.

Thoughts about himself and his relationship with Judy nagged at Michael as he sat there alone wondering what was happening. He didn't know how to help himself: all he wanted to do was wake up and get on with things. He got out of bed and took a hot and then a cold shower. When he slipped back under the heavy quilt it was 7:15 A.M. and the alarm clock was ringing. As Judy reached over and turned it off, Michael snuggled next to her warm body. She held him close and they kissed. Her body felt good and reassuring to him; his pestering thoughts about himself and their relationship vanished. He got more excited. As they made love without talking, Michael knew he would be a little late for work.

Jobs and reality were pressing. Michael and Judy both

dressed quickly and went their separate ways. As Michael drove to work, the Dream Maker was there, tripping him up, challenging his pictures about his life, trying to take Michael back closer to what had happened during sleep. Michael tried to think of his coming workday. The fight inside of him would become a running battle—Michael fighting to maintain his position and the Dream Maker questioning, pushing, reminding, and shifting him to new ground. Michael kept retreating; he was unable to stop it all from happening.

He couldn't remember but at times he tried. Was it a thought, a dream, a memory? Michael's head was a jumble of confusion. All he knew was that "something was happening."


Time passed for Michael. It had been over four days since his encounter with the Dream Maker. He had said nothing to anyone, but a few of his close friends, especially Judy, noticed that he had changed. He was not as outgoing, not as sure of himself, not as cocky as before.

Judy was facing her own crisis. It was happening again; she could feel it. Something was wrong between them. She thought she might be losing the man she loved. That thought wasn't new. It had happened to her before. She couldn't decide what was wrong with her. She was five pounds overweight, but her figure was still good and firm. She liked sex, even though at times she pretended a little. She really tried to make the relationship work. Judy felt sad and often cried alone which made her feel worse and better. She pulled herself together because she was determined to have a talk with him; she didn't want to lose one more time.

Judy had something special—an earthiness that kept her close to what she really wanted. She could still feel that she wanted more in life. She really wanted a life with Michael. On Friday she got home twenty minutes ahead of Michael and hurried to straighten up and start their dinner. She tried to make it nice, this place where they lived.

When Michael came in, they kissed, but not really. They both knew something was off between them. Judy decided to wait, but then she just blurted it out—all her thoughts and worries. She cried. Michael had seen her cry before, but this time he did not pull away as he usually did. Michael felt bad himself. He was glad she was crying; he wished he could.

They talked over dinner, and late into the night. For the first time—they really talked. They stumbled for the right words and often didn't find them, but they were trying. They both knew they had reached their bottom line. They didn't want to pass things over this time, or to move on to other relationships. They both felt too bad and too much. Michael told Judy about his "bad night" and how it had affected him all week. They had begun a very slow initiation into becoming Dream Makers.

The Dream Maker in Michael had begun to emerge. There were going to be more battles, retreats, losses, and victories, but it was happening.

Judy and Michael were lucky because they had the chance to begin facing themselves—and they did. They were also lucky in that they just stumbled into getting help for themselves; otherwise they would have had to "go it" on instinct alone.

The two of them used to rush around on Saturdays trying to get their endless errands done. But today, they just sat and ate a leisurely brunch. Michael read the sports section while Judy followed the adventures of B.C. in the comic strips. By about two in the afternoon both of them had read almost the entire paper.

"Michael, did you read that ad for the lecture on dreams?"

"Yeah, it sounded interesting."

"Do you want to go?"

"I don't know, I thought maybe we'd just stay home and rest."

The Dream Maker was there. Michael thought about the lecture and remembered his dreams, "You know, Judy, I would like to go."

Michael called the listed number.

"Forest Hospital."

"I don't know if I have the right number. I want information about the Dream Maker lecture?"

He did have the right number and soon Michael had made reservations for two. As he wrote down the instructions he thought about going to a hospital to hear a lecture. It frightened him a little, but his dream and what had happened to him scared him even more.

The drive to the hospital was pleasant; Michael and Judy talked excitedly about their dreams. There were about a hundred people at the lecture. At exactly the announced time, two handsome men walked onto the stage. Everyone was set for a serious opening. But one of these doctors was making funny noises into the microphone. The early tension in the room cracked.

"Thank you for coming tonight. . . ." What happened in the next two hours seemed like a dream itself. The young psychologists filled the room with talk.

"You dream the way you live and you live the way you dream. . . . Everyone has a nighttime psychotherapist who tries to help you with your feelings—we call this nighttime guide the Dream Maker. . . ."

Before Judy and Michael had time to ask all the questions they had prepared on the ride to the hospital the lecture was over. They sat there quietly as people filed out.

"You know I feel like I've just been to a magic show. The way they talk, and act, and move is exciting."

"Michael, I think our dreams are really close to what they are talking about, even some of our really simple dreams."

Three months after attending the lecture, Michael and Judy received an announcement which was an invitation to attend a forthcoming Dream Maker workshop that would be held in Chicago. They talked it over at length. They liked what they had heard at the lecture; it had helped them understand and live from their dreams more clearly, and they wanted more. "But would it be worth it: Would anything really change?" Michael questioned.

What finally decided it for them was Judy's plan—"Look, we can make a vacation of it. We'll go to the hotel early and stay a day after the workshop is over."

They preregistered by mail for the workshop and a week later received an information packet. The first thing they read in the packet was a mimeographed handout:

> The meetings and groups you will attend are not intended to be encounter groups or psychotherapy sessions. Nobody will force you to talk or ask you to do anything you don't want to do. We are just extending to you the same invitation your Dream Maker gives you every night: see the pictures of your life, feel the pictures, see what you can change and begin to change what you want.

"Hey, look at this," said Judy. "It says don't open anything else in this packet except the envelope marked 'Friday Night Instructions.' What is this supposed to be, Clue-a-Night?"

"Well," joked Michael, "you know the little old Dream Maker will get you if you don't watch out."

He was right. The purpose of the Dream Maker workshop was to help people meet their own Dream Maker. The envelopes they opened contained the same message for both of them:

> On the morning of the workshop, write down whatever dreams you remember. If you don't remember a dream, write down your thoughts and feelings. Sweet dreams.

## The First Meeting

"There is a big difference between becoming a Dream Maker and having a Dream Maker. Everyone has a Dream Maker who is at work every night making dreams. Only a few people become Dream Makers. The Dream Maker awakens you to your dreams; becoming a Dream Maker means staying awake."

It was the first meeting; Jerry and Lee, two of the four group leaders, were talking to all the workshop participants in a big meeting room. Michael and Judy sat in the front row of the semicircle, looking closely and listening to the two men.

"Your dream pictures are clearer than our words," they said. "If you are looking on in your dreams and they just seem to happen, then you are not a Dream Maker. But if you are feeling and moving and expressing yourself fully then you and the Dream Maker are one—you are the Dream Maker.

"You will know when the Dream Maker visits you with a Breakthru Dream. But you may not know that the Dream Maker has done nothing more than show you your life as it could be, at its fullest.

"In ancient times people labeled such visits as 'visitations from the gods.' They hoped and prayed that the gods would send them a dream to guide their lives. They did receive Breakthru Dreams, but few people became Dream Makers because they continued to believe the Dream Maker was outside themselves. Becoming a Dream Maker means accepting who you are. . . .

"We could tell you much more, but what we tell you will be less important this weekend than what you learn from your own dreams. You can't become a Dream Maker by memorizing words about dreams."

The sixty people in the room were then divided into groups of fifteen, each with a different group leader. Judy ended up in a group with Riggs, while Michael went with Joe's group. They both felt a little more anxious when separated.

## JUDY'S FIRST GROUP

Judy was glad she would be in Riggs's group. She had liked him right from the start because he too liked to joke and laugh a lot; she felt safer with a Dream Maker who laughed.

The room they went into was fairly small, had thick brown

carpet on the floor, and only one chair. Riggs asked everyone to lie down and close their eyes. He made sure each person had room to move about and then began to talk, softly and slowly:

"I want you to just listen for a few minutes. I'm going to tell you one of the most important things you can ever learn about your dreams. *A dream is a picture of a feeling. A dream is a picture of a feeling. A dream is a picture of a feeling.*

"You don't have to figure out your dreams; they aren't coded messages that need to be deciphered. Your dreams picture your feelings. The way to use your dreams is to feel the pictures. Some of the dream pictures will feel good and some will feel bad. Some will be confused and hard to feel. But all your dream pictures are important because they are all about you and your life; they show you how your life feels.

"Okay, take a minute now and just go over a dream you had this morning. Don't try to understand it, just let yourself feel the pictures."

He waited, about five minutes, and then asked, "Does anyone want to tell their dream?"

Judy wanted to, but it wasn't a super dream—certainly not the big dream she had hoped for. She had already told the dream to Michael that morning and Michael had just passed it over with, "Well, I don't know."

Judy had a hard time listening as others in her group told their dreams. She really wanted to talk, but felt too shy. She began to relax as she listened to Riggs helping the others. He told another woman, "Every dream you remember is important. Just being able to remember your feelings is worthwhile. The way to have Breakthru Dreams is to have little dreams first, really *have* them and share them and feel what they are showing you."

Just as Riggs finished, maybe even a little before, with a little stutter Judy said she wanted to tell her dream and began, "Well, I was coming to a river, a big river. There were plants along the river I had never seen before. I asked my boyfriend Michael to look at the plants with me, but he didn't want to; he wanted to go swimming. I looked at the plants by myself and found some that were flowering. Then I woke up."

Riggs smiled and looked at her, "How did you feel coming to the river?"

"Oh, I was very excited and a little scared. The plants were beautiful and fascinating. I just wanted to look and look all over the place. But I felt frustrated that Michael wouldn't look with me."

"Have you felt that way with Michael before?" Riggs asked.

Judy knew that she had, often, but she felt a little embarrassed to mention it, "Well, yes . . ."

"That's the feeling you're picturing in your dream. Do you want to talk more about it?" Riggs moved closer to her.

"Uh-huh, but it's kind of embarrassing. Sometimes I want to talk about things and Michael just wants to have sex. I don't feel good if I go ahead and have sex without talking."

"How do you feel in the dream when you look around and see the flowers?"

Judy answered, "Oh, really wonderful. I feel delicate and just right."

Riggs spoke gently to her, "Let's summarize what you know. You feel good when you take the time to really look at the delicate flowers and you feel frustrated when Michael doesn't. And this all feels similar to what happens when you have sex. What is important here is not just the specific thing you remember but how you feel. It feels bad to you to not take time. This dream is trying to teach you to take the time."

Riggs and Judy continued to talk for half an hour, and he helped her feel the pictures in her dream. Then he spoke to everyone in the room: "You can take the Dream Maker Approach to your dreams and your life long before you have a Breakthru Dream. Just keep in mind that your dreams picture your feelings and your dreams show you both the old pictures you have been living and the new pictures you could live."

The first group ended about ten minutes later. Judy felt good; she had half hoped and half feared that something dramatic and urgent would come out of the meeting for her, but what she had instead was a small glow. She felt hopeful she would be able to change and it wouldn't be gigantic and painful.


## MICHAEL'S FIRST GROUP

Michael's group met with their leader, Joe, in a room almost like the one Judy was meeting in except it had an orange carpet and a window looking out on Lake Michigan. Joe asked everyone to sit against the walls; then he sat in the middle and talked: "The Dream Maker makes pictures of feelings. To take the Dream Maker Approach to your dreams, just recognize that *your* pictures in *your* dreams are *your* feelings. If you make and live one picture, you can also make and live another picture. No one is trapped. Even if you have a dream that pictures you caught in a trap, you made the picture to describe your life and you can change the picture by changing your life.

"To take the Dream Maker Approach, realize that the pictures are of your life and you can change how you are in the pictures."

Michael spoke up right away, "I know I really felt trapped in my dream; I couldn't get away and it felt awful.

"I was in an old tenement building like some I've seen in the slums of Chicago. The furniture in my apartment was old, not at all like my real furniture. Everything smelled musty and unpleasant. I was sitting in a rocker and I looked like an old woman. I just rocked back and forth."

Joe began to help Michael feel more about his dream. "Michael, what I'm going to teach you now we call the Picture Technique. First, ask yourself, 'How do the pictures in my dream feel to me?' "

Michael answered, "They feel terrible; I don't want to be there at all; I can't stand to just sit there in that rocking chair."

"Next, ask yourself, 'When have I felt that way before?' "

Michael didn't hesitate, "I get the same feeling whenever I just wait around, especially at work. I work as an insurance claims adjuster and it seems like I spend half my time waiting around."

"Next, say to yourself, 'This picture is my life.' "

"No, I don't want to say that. I want to change the picture. I want to get up out of the rocking chair and out of that old apartment."

Joe said to him, "You need to own the pictures and the feelings first, otherwise you would have changed them already."

"It seems terrible to say."

But Michael took a little chance and as he did he began to feel more, "It's terrible. I just keep waiting and waiting."

Michael was taking the first difficult step toward becoming a Dream Maker. He was feeling his life as it really was. Words about wanting more time and wanting to play more seemed pale and shallow compared to the pictures in his dream. His pictures shook his body; they affected him. By taking his dream pictures seriously, Michael was aligning himself with the Dream Maker who wanted him to take his life seriously.

Joe talked more to the group. Sometimes he sounded ordinary and sometimes, Michael felt, Joe's words came to him like his own dream pictures—shaking his beliefs and certainties. "You know the choice is always there. You can live from new movements and new pictures or old movements and old pictures. Right this moment each of you is choosing to not listen or listen, to not talk or talk, to hide yourself or show yourself. You are choosing whether you will feel good or feel bad. You are letting your feelings work for you or against you."

Michael could feel inside himself that ebb and flow of choosing and knowing. He worried that he would not be strong enough to know to choose.


The group leaders had instructed everyone to take a look at the workshop packets and read what was in the envelopes before coming back at 11:30 A.M. for a meeting. One mimeographed sheet said:

## QUESTIONS AND MORE QUESTIONS AND A FEW ANSWERS

As we puzzled about the Dream Maker we came up with many questions. Some of them seem a little silly now, but we want you to know how we were thinking. Here are a few:

What is the shape of the Dream Maker?
What is the age of the Dream Maker?
What is the purpose of the Dream Maker?
What does the Dream Maker do during the day?
Is the Dream Maker ever wrong?
Does the Dream Maker really exist?
How do you recognize a Dream Maker if you see one?
Why don't we have Breakthru Dreams every night?

All the answers to these questions came out of talks that followed dreams. We didn't sit down and generate answers theoretically.

## SOME ANSWERS

The Dream Maker has no fixed shape. It can take any shape and make any picture. We can't say, "If you dream of an old man or a unicorn or a talking mountain, you are seeing the Dream Maker."

The Dream Maker has no fixed age. It is our past, our present, and our future all at once. The Dream Maker's pictures show the influences of our past, the needs we have in the present and the possibilities of the future.

The purpose of the Dream Maker is to picture our lives. Becoming a Dream Maker means taking over which pictures we live.

The Dream Maker doesn't sleep. It is awake night and day. But the perceptions and routines of the day usually block the pictures the Dream Maker can give.

In the domain of the Dream Maker there is no right or wrong. There is only what is or was or could be.

The Dream Maker really exists in the same sense our feelings really exist.

Dream Makers can recognize one another because they see underneath pictures. If you don't know you are making pictures, then you can't know another Dream Maker.

We have the dreams we are willing to live. If we are willing to live intensely, clearly and fully every day, then we will have many Breakthru Dreams; if we live in confusion, then our dreams picture that confusion.

"You know," said Michael, "I'm sure now that I was having a Dream Maker dream months ago when I got so scared."

"I think so too," said Judy.

Michael looked unhappy with himself. "I wish I could remember what it was. It says something about me that I would have a big dream and then forget it."

"You didn't forget the feeling, Michael. Our whole life started to change because you didn't forget how you felt."

"Yeah, that's right, I guess I just want more." Michael didn't sound altogether sure.

In the world of the Dream Maker what you want is what you get. Michael's wants were beginning to be less censored and he was starting to let himself expand toward new feelings. When that happens people often feel less sure of themselves for a time.

When the sixty people got back together before lunch, there was a noticeable change in the big group. Most of the nervousness was gone, but there was more visible excitement.

Jerry started right out: "The easiest way to let you know about the Breakthru Dream and the Dream Maker would be to conjure up for you a powerful, life-changing dream. But we can't do that. You have your own Dream Maker; and it's a good thing because we don't know your life. The dreams we would make for you would be imitations of our own dreams or those of our friends. They wouldn't fit you; they wouldn't show you true pictures of your feelings and your possibilities."

Riggs added, "The Dream Maker is like a personal therapist everyone has inside himself. Each night the Dream Maker runs his free therapy session and gives you the chance to see your life and make some changes in the way you left things. The Dream Maker gives second chances to go over things that you leave incomplete; sometimes it gives third and fourth and fifty-second chances."

Judy and Michael could both understand more clearly what the speakers were saying after their morning's experiences. Judy, especially, felt that Riggs had given her at least a dozen chances to feel how she wanted to live with Michael.

Riggs was talking, "Like a wise therapist, the Dream Maker shows you only what you can see. If you are not ready to feel and live from a Breakthru Dream the Dream Maker will make for you those dreams that will ease tensions and give a few insights. If you are ready, but unwilling, the Dream Maker may scare you with a few nightmares to bring you back to the urgency of your life. Whenever it can be done, the invitation will be made to enter the Dream Maker Tradition and become a Dream Maker yourself."

Joe added, "Actually it is very simple to say how to become a Dream Maker instead of continuing to be a person who has dreams: *live your feelings fully*. The Dream Maker is your connection to who you really are and how you really feel beneath all the roles and games and reasonable ways to do things."

Judy knew she wanted to live differently with Michael. She also knew that when she followed her feelings she felt good and when she didn't she felt miserable.

The speakers continued: "This afternoon your group leaders will go back over the same dreams you talked about this morning and help you to see even more clearly how your dreams are pictures of your feelings and how to take the first steps of the Dream Maker Approach to your dreams."

After the workshop, when the participants had left the meeting hall to go to lunch, Riggs said to Joe, "You know, I'm always surprised that people can begin to respond so quickly to their dreams."

"I understand it," said Joe. "It's easier for people to respond to their own dreams than to something someone else says. Look at Michael, if I told him that he was bored with his job he'd resist me; but when he can see pictures of himself as an old woman in a rocking chair then he gets the feeling without struggling. It's his dream, not mine."

"Yeah, I think he'll really be able to live from his feelings. You know, Judy and Michael could really help each other."

Michael might have been happy to hear them talking because, just then, he was not so optimistic.

# 13
# The What, Why, and How of Dreaming

## The Second Meeting

The afternoon group began at 1:30 P.M. Jerry, Lee, Riggs, and Joe all talked in a kind of tag-team lecture format. When one of them stopped talking, another immediately picked up and continued the same theme. It was like listening to a story or listening in on a conversation.

"This afternoon we'll talk just a short while and then we want to show you a film which shows one of our therapists, Dominic, helping another therapist, Steve, with his dream. The film will show you an extension of the Picture Technique you learned today. The extension we call the Make-It-Work Technique. But before you can understand that way of working with dreams you need to understand a bit more about what dreams are and what they can be.

"Here's our first teaching: *A dream is a picture of a feeling.* That's *what* a dream is. The picture may be confusing, mixed-up and inconsistent; or it may be clear, direct, and full of feeling. The pictures we dream are in the same condition as our feelings. People whose feelings are clear dream clearly; mixed-up people dream mixed-up dreams."

"That's me," whispered Michael.

Judy inwardly flinched, but just looked at him. There was a tone in his "that's me" that scared her. She started to regret coming to the workshop. Sometimes when Michael got upset he would be moody for days and days. Maybe the workshop was going to upset their relationship.

The maybes came faster and faster. All of a sudden she didn't like the hotel or the carpets or the seats they were sitting in. She didn't like her dreams or what happened this morning. The Dream Maker was there. He was turning her waking into a nightmare.

Michael wasn't upset with Judy or anyone else; he wanted to talk more. The Dream Maker had gotten to him again, but this time there was no big scary dream. This Joe, this therapist from Los Angeles, seemed as if he had a wiretap to Michael's thoughts. Michael wished he had really let Joe know how much he wanted to let out what was bottled up inside.

Michael didn't know what was happening; all that he was sure of was that "something was happening." He felt a strong urge to talk, to interrupt, to let Joe know what he had been through in his life.

"Here is our *second* teaching about dreams: *Dreams attempt to complete feelings left incomplete during the day or in the past*. In a way dreams give us a second chance.

"The *why* of dreaming is this: We dream to restore the balance of our lives. Dreams are attempts to complete feelings which were left incomplete. For thousands of years people have tried to understand dreams, interpret them, find their meanings. That's not what we do in the Dream Maker Approach. Instead we try to make dreams work.

"Here is our third teaching: *A Breakthru Dream is a dream that works*. A dream that works is *always* expressive, feelingful, and realistically connected to your life. That is the *how* of dreaming.

"Dreams that don't work are malfunctioning—the dreamer may be passive instead of expressively active, the dream feeling may be flat, the dream may be symbolic and confused.

"Now that we've told you something about the *what*, *why*, and *how* of dreaming, we want to show you more about how dreams can be made to work."

For the next forty-five minutes the audience watched a film showing Dominic helping Steve. The intensity of feeling and expression in the film affected everyone. It was like watching a nightmare change into a "daymare" and then change to pure pleasure.

The speakers didn't answer more questions after the film. Instead, they told everyone: "Don't try to figure this out. Just let yourself be affected. If you do, this film will enter your dreams tonight."

Michael was not at all sure he wanted that experience in his dreams. He felt on the edge already—of what he wasn't sure.

## The Dream Test

Next there was a change of pace in the workshop. Everyone took a short dream test called the Dream Capabilities Assessment Test (DCAT). Jerry introduced the test by saying: "The Breakthru Dream and the Dream Maker Process you've been hearing about taught us to ask different questions about dreams. These questions are focused not on what a dream means but on how a dream works. We want you to go through a short dream test with us now so that you will begin to get an idea of how your dreams work or don't work and from there begin to learn how to make your dreams work better."

# THE DREAM CAPABILITIES ASSESSMENT TEST*

**Instructions:**

1. Work quickly through the entire test. It should take approximately 12 minutes. Since there are no correct answers, answer from your first impulse or impression.

2. Simply fill in the appropriate space for your answer. Be sure not to omit any questions. For example, if you choose answer #3, then blacken the space under the column headed "3".

3. Remember, all questions (unless otherwise specified) are about the way you generally dream. Take into consideration your dreams over the last year. ☞

1. How often do you remember your dreams?
   (1) never (2) once or twice a year (3) a couple of times a month (4) two to four times a week (5) one or more dreams every night

   | 1 | 2 | 3 | 4 | 5 |
   |---|---|---|---|---|
   | ☐ | ☐ | ☐ | ☐ | ☐ |

2. Do you ever think about your dreams even if you don't remember them?
   (1) not at all (2) infrequently (3) sometimes (4) frequently

   | 1 | 2 | 3 | 4 |
   |---|---|---|---|
   | ☐ | ☐ | ☐ | ☐ |

3. Do you ever wake up in the morning and feel as if you have been through something meaningful, powerful, or frightening but just can't remember what happened?
   (1) never (2) infrequently (3) sometimes (4) frequently

   | 1 | 2 | 3 | 4 |
   |---|---|---|---|
   | ☐ | ☐ | ☐ | ☐ |

4. Does a dream memory or feeling linger with you throughout the day—seeming to pop up because someone says something to you or you see something that triggers a reminder?
   (1) never (2) infrequently (3) sometimes (4) frequently

   | 1 | 2 | 3 | 4 |
   |---|---|---|---|
   | ☐ | ☐ | ☐ | ☐ |

5. Do you ever talk about your dreams to your friends?
   (1) never (2) infrequently (3) sometimes (4) frequently

   | 1 | 2 | 3 | 4 |
   |---|---|---|---|
   | ☐ | ☐ | ☐ | ☐ |

6. Do you ever write your dreams down?
   (1) never (2) infrequently (3) sometimes (4) frequently

   | 1 | 2 | 3 | 4 |
   |---|---|---|---|
   | ☐ | ☐ | ☐ | ☐ |

7. Generally, how long does it take you to get to sleep?
   (1) not able to get to sleep without medica-

tion (2) one hour or more (3) 30 minutes to
one hour (4) 15 to 30 minutes (5) 15 minutes
or less

|   | 1 | 2 | 3 | 4 | 5 |
|---|---|---|---|---|---|
|   | □ | □ | □ | □ | □ |

8. Generally, how do you usually feel when
you awake in the morning?
(1) sluggish (2) awake but tired (3) awake
(4) awake and alert (5) awake and
pleasantly alert

|   | 1 | 2 | 3 | 4 | 5 |
|---|---|---|---|---|---|
|   | □ | □ | □ | □ | □ |

9. Do you ever have repetitive dreams?
(1) frequently (2) sometimes (3) infrequently
(4) never

|   | 1 | 2 | 3 | 4 |
|---|---|---|---|---|
|   | □ | □ | □ | □ |

10. Do you ever have nightmares?
(1) never (2) infrequently (3) sometimes
(4) frequently

|   | 1 | 2 | 3 | 4 |
|---|---|---|---|---|
|   | □ | □ | □ | □ |

11. Do you dream in color?
(1) no awareness of color (2) mostly black
and white (3) some color (4) mostly color
(5) vivid, intense color

|   | 1 | 2 | 3 | 4 | 5 |
|---|---|---|---|---|---|
|   | □ | □ | □ | □ | □ |

12. Overall, how would you rate your dreams?
(1) symbolic (Requires interpretation to understand. Dream makes an indirect statement about dreamer's life.)
(2) mostly symbolic
(3) mixture of symbolic and real (There are
real and symbolic parts to the dream picture.)
(4) mostly real
(5) real (A nonsymbolic picture about the
dreamer's life—either past or present—
where there is direct expression of feelings,
thoughts, and actions.)

|   | 1 | 2 | 3 | 4 | 5 |
|---|---|---|---|---|---|
|   | □ | □ | □ | □ | □ |

13. What kind of characters usually appear in your dreams?
(1) no characters at all (The dreamer is not even in the dream.)
(2) no other characters (The dreamer is alone in the dream.)
(3) unknown (Not personally known, including famous people, monsters, animals, strangers.)
(4) both (Both known and unknown characters.)
(5) known (Personally known characters in dreams. The characters are the same as they are in waking life—including animals.)

1 2 3 4 5
☐ ☐ ☐ ☐ ☐

14. On the average, how would you rate your satisfaction level in your dreams?
(1) completely dissatisfied (The dream picture is incomplete. There is a sense that the dream is unfinished.)
(2) somewhat dissatisfied
(3) somewhat satisfied (In one aspect the dream is complete, but the dreamer could have done more to complete the story.)
(4) completely satisfied (The picture and story are complete. The dreamer feels finished with the total dream.)

1 2 3 4
☐ ☐ ☐ ☐

15. Generally, taking all of your dreams into consideration, how active are you in your dreams?
(1) no role (The dreamer has no role in the dreams.)
(2) passive (The dreamer is only a part of the dreams. His role is that of being present but

uninvolved and unresponsive.)
(3) slightly active (There is some response
by the dreamer to dream events, but for the
most part the dreamer's role does not
change the outcome of the dreams.)
(4) active (Dreamer's activity is obvious. His
role in response to events is complete.)
(5) very active (Dreamer's activity dominates
the dreams.)

1 2 3 4 5
☐ ☐ ☐ ☐ ☐

16. Generally, how expressive are you in your
dreams?
(1) no expression (No outward manifestation
of any type of dreamer expression of feelings
or thoughts.)
(2) slight (Some expression, but relegated to
a minor feature.)
(3) moderate (Definite but not striking expression.)
(4) strong (Expression takes preference over
all other dreamer activities, but does not
dominate dreams.)
(5) intense (Prolonged and complete expression of feeling. Expression dominates entire
dreams, even in the face of obstacles.)

1 2 3 4 5
☐ ☐ ☐ ☐ ☐

17. Generally, how much feeling do you have in
your dreams?
(1) no feeling (Dreams about things or
events that remain neutral.)
(2) slight (The dreams evoke some feeling;
the feeling though is vague and in
the background.)
(3) moderate (There is some feeling that is
not vague, but it does not dominate or even
greatly influence the dreams.)

(4) strong (Definite feeling, more than is usually evident in normal waking life, but it does not dominate entire dreams.)
(5) intense (The feeling overrides all else in dreams. The dreamer is aware that he is feeling and allows it to fully occur.)

1 2 3 4 5
☐ ☐ ☐ ☐ ☐

18. Generally, how much clarity do you have in your dreams?
(1) completely confused (The dream pictures are incoherent. Events and feelings have no relationship.)
(2) unclear and indirect (There is much distortion, though it does not completely obscure the dream pictures.)
(3) somewhat clear and direct (There is a general idea of what is going on in the dreams. Some elements may be distorted.)
(4) clear and direct (The pictures are clear and direct but not complete.)
(5) completely clear and direct (Feelings and actions are totally clear and direct. There is no distortion.)

1 2 3 4 5
☐ ☐ ☐ ☐ ☐

19. Do you ever have a dream in which you can do powerful, or extraordinary feats?
(1) never (2) once (3) infrequently (4) sometimes (5) frequently

1 2 3 4 5
☐ ☐ ☐ ☐ ☐

20. Do you ever have a dream in which you express your feelings through words, sounds, and actions so that you dominate the dream completely?
(1) never (2) once (3) infrequently (4) sometimes (5) frequently

1 2 3 4 5
☐ ☐ ☐ ☐ ☐

21. Do you ever have a dream in which you have full feeling so intense that it becomes a reference for the rest of your life?
(1) never (2) once (3) infrequently
(4) sometimes (5) frequently

1 2 3 4 5
☐ ☐ ☐ ☐ ☐

22. Do you ever have a dream in which there is super-awareness so that it is completely clear and vivid; a dream with no symbolism, a direct message or vision; nothing is disguised or distorted?
(1) never (2) once (3) infrequently
(4) sometimes (5) frequently

1 2 3 4 5
☐ ☐ ☐ ☐ ☐

23. Do you ever have a dream in which you shift from passive to active, and/or from confused to clear, and/or from no feeling to full feeling, and/or from non-expressive to fully expressive?
(1) never (2) once (3) infrequently
(4) sometimes (5) frequently

1 2 3 4 5
☐ ☐ ☐ ☐ ☐

24. Have you ever had dreams that were completely clear, where you were totally powerful, expressive and moving; dreams with intense feeling and bright, vivid colors; dreams where all of these things came together with shifts from symbolic to real?
(1) never (2) once (3) infrequently
(4) sometimes (5) frequently

1 2 3 4 5
☐ ☐ ☐ ☐ ☐

25. Do you have dreams that you cannot forget? That stay with you all your life?
(1) never (2) once (3) infrequently
(4) sometimes (5) frequently

1 2 3 4 5
☐ ☐ ☐ ☐ ☐

26. Do you ever clearly re-experience your past, feeling and expressing what you couldn't as a child?
    (1) never (2) infrequently (3) sometimes (4) frequently

    | 1 | 2 | 3 | 4 |
    |---|---|---|---|
    | □ | □ | □ | □ |

27. Do you ever clearly re-experience your present, feeling and expressing what you didn't in a certain situation?
    (1) never (2) infrequently (3) sometimes (4) frequently

    | 1 | 2 | 3 | 4 |
    |---|---|---|---|
    | □ | □ | □ | □ |

28. Do your friends ever help you in your dreams?
    (1) never (2) infrequently (3) sometimes (4) frequently

    | 1 | 2 | 3 | 4 |
    |---|---|---|---|
    | □ | □ | □ | □ |

29. Do you ever have dreams that tell you what you need to do in the future?
    (1) never (2) infrequently (3) sometimes (4) frequently

    | 1 | 2 | 3 | 4 |
    |---|---|---|---|
    | □ | □ | □ | □ |

30. Have your dreams changed over the last two years?
    (1) no (2) yes

    | 1 | 2 |
    |---|---|
    | □ | □ |

31. Do your dreams ever seem to teach you something directly; something that doesn't need any explanation or interpretation?
    (1) never (2) infrequently (3) sometimes (4) frequently

    | 1 | 2 | 3 | 4 |
    |---|---|---|---|
    | □ | □ | □ | □ |

32. Would you like your dreams to change?
    (1) no (2) yes

    | 1 | 2 |
    |---|---|
    | □ | □ |

33. How would you rate your awareness while
you are dreaming?
(1) unaware (You are dreaming and you do
not know it. You act in the dream only as a
participant.)
(2) partially aware (You realize you are
dreaming or you are having a dream, but
you can't do anything about it. You don't
have a solid point of reference while
dreaming.)
(3) aware (You are aware of yourself as a
dreamer. You act in the dream because you
can see what is happening, but you do not
have an outside reference. You don't know
you are dreaming.
(4) completely aware (You realize while you
are sleeping that you are dreaming. You
have a separate dream viewpoint. You are
able to have realizations in the dream that
allow you to change your behavior. You recognize that you are feeling a certain way
and you respond to it.

1 2 3 4
□ □ □ □

## SCORING THE TEST

In actuality there are two ways to score the Dream CAT. The simplest way is to add up the numerical values of your answers. There are a total of thirty-three questions and a minimum score of thirty-three. Once you have your score then go to the graph titled "Dream Capabilities Assessment Profile," and place your score in the appropriate position on the graph. This will give you a visual representation of your Dream Capability. Below the graph you will find a range of scores and an explanation for each range.

# DREAM CAPABILITY
# ASSESSMENT PROFILE*

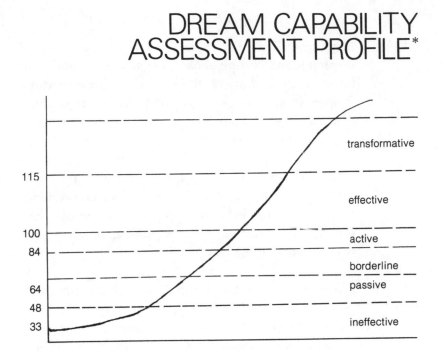

33–47    *Ineffective.* Your dreams do not work for you. The
         dreams you experience are from old static images with
         little energy, power, feeling or clarity. Your dreams
         are generally symbolic and fragmented. You are ignor-
         ing the one-third of your life that you spend sleeping
         and dreaming. You need to move out of your old way
         of dreaming.

48–63    *Passive.* Your scores show that you have some aware-
         ness of your dreams. You sometimes, but not always,
         pay attention to your dreams. Your dreams are usually
         unsatisfying. The old dream images and old way of
         dreaming predominate. You need to get more in-
         volved in your dream life.

64–83   *Borderline.* This is a critical place. Your old way of dreaming and the symbolic images are beginning to break down. You are on the edge of having something happen in your dreams. If you make some changes your dreams can start working for you. Your dreams can have more color, action, expression, and feeling.

84–97   *Active.* The old dream images are ready to be transformed. Your dreams can be used as an inner guide, moving you towards more feeling, awareness, and clarity. You need to keep expanding to start your dreams working for you.

100–114   *Effective.* Out of the symbolism and old images a powerful new dream force is ready to emerge. With some help you can expect to experience significant shifts in your dreams. Your dreams are ready to affect your life.

115+   *Transformative.* You are becoming a new kind of dreamer. The old symbolic images have given way to new dreams. A dream force can continue to emerge and expand and move you toward dreaming with full awareness, feeling, power, and clarity.


The scoring you have just completed is the simplest and used only for explanatory purposes. If you wish a detailed score and evaluation of your test, make a copy of the entire test with your marked answers and send to:

DREAM RESEARCH PROJECT
THE CENTER FOUNDATION
7165 Sunset Blvd.
Los Angeles, California 90028

You will receive free of charge by return mail a more detailed analysis of your Dream CAT. (Be sure to enclose a stamped, self-addressed envelope.) Your scores will be added to the data bank we are collecting on dream capabilities. For more information on our dream research see Appendixes A and B.

It took an hour for everyone in the group to take the DCAT, score their tests, and graph the results. All the participants went over their own scores and Riggs helped interpret them. A participant asked a question about her score of 81 on the Dream Capability Assessment Profile: "If I don't move up on this scale will I go down?"

Riggs said, "Yes, you are at a critical transitional place. You'll learn more about what you can do when we talk about the Dream Maker processes."

He went on, "Your scores for Graph 1 are pretty self-explanatory. The main idea to keep in mind is that at one time you were all dream geniuses. Once upon a time as children you would all have scored at the top of the scale. Since then your natural abilities have been scaled down."

The four group leaders then met with their groups to help everyone understand what their scores and graphs meant.

That afternoon Judy was in Jerry's group and she listened to him explain, "Feelings are your inner climate or weather and dreams are like weather reports. They tell you what's been happening and what is likely to happen with your feelings. These graphs from the DCAT are like weather summaries. We have identified the most important influences that combine together to make up your dreams. These are: Expression, Feeling Level, Clarity, and Activity. These are what go together to make up the Dream Maker Process. When they are high you will have Breakthru Dreams. When they are low, your Dream Maker is being held back by your Censor."

Bob, a New York City jeweler, was in the same group as

Judy. He was not happy about his scores. He began to argue with Jerry about whether the scores really showed anything about his feelings.

Jerry answered him, "It's easy to argue with me or with another therapist or leader, but do you want to argue with what your own dreams are telling you about yourself? You are the one who has to live in the climate you make. Once you accept what your dreams are telling you then you can begin to listen to how they tell you to change."

Bob said, "I guess I'm disappointed. I've always been interested in understanding dreams and I'm surprised that I didn't get a higher score."

"You know, Bob, you can understand your dreams perfectly but they still won't change. Understanding or interpreting is a kind of postdream effort that people get into to undo the work of the Censor. What we are emphasizing is different. We want you to recognize what you can do to be on the side of the Dream Maker."

Judy was pleased with her scores. They were not all that high, but she could see clearly that to change her dreams she needed to bring her expressiveness and activity up to her feeling level.

## MICHAEL'S AFTERNOON GROUP

Joe was waiting for Michael. He knew that he had gotten to him. As the group gathered in the smaller meeting room, Joe sat silently waiting. Everyone was sitting around when he said, "Some of you think that your dreams are a sleepy time story—a nighttime entertainment. You're wrong."

Michael was dying inside; Joe was doing it again, talking directly to him. Joe looked at Michael and then went on. "When you dabble with your dreams you are playing a very serious game of Russian roulette. Without knowing it, you could blow you own head off with your dreams. Dreams are some of the most profound and emotional powder kegs that you can experience. Some of you came here really needing to talk; if you don't, you are better off leaving right now. There are others in here who don't really need to talk at all; you need to listen and learn. Each one of you needs to answer that question for yourself— what do you need to do?"

Michael knew what he needed. "Joe, I need to talk more about my dream. I need to talk right now."

Joe said, "Let's try the Make-It-Work Technique with your dream, Michael."

Joe spoke to the whole group: "You can make your dreams work *during* a dream or *after* a dream. These two kinds of dream work are tied together. If you begin to make your dreams work now, you will feel different. When you feel different during the day then your dream pictures will become different at night."

"Okay, Michael, tell us your dream again. Let us hear it just the way it felt to you when you were dreaming."

Michael retold his dream; he again became a little red-faced when he described himself "looking like an old woman."

"If we pick out just one picture from your dream, you in the rocking chair, how do you feel in that picture?"

Michael answered, "I feel terrible but I just keep rocking."

"Do you have that same feeling at other times in your life outside the dream?"

"Yeah, I told you before I feel that way all the time at work. Most of the day I just kill time."

Joe spoke quietly to him, "Now let's take just one process in the dream—your activity—and change it some. What would you do if you could?"

At this Michael began to get agitated. He yelled, "I'd get out of that damn rocker and smash it to pieces."

"Go ahead, make that movement. Imagine you're smashing the rocker!" Michael began to really move around the room. He seemed to have a hundred old rockers that needed smashing.

"Now say something when you smash the rockers!"

Michael yelled out, "I don't want to stay here. I'm leaving. I'm getting out. I want more."

As he said these words his feeling began to shift. He became less frantic and more solid. He began to sound surer and stronger.

He spoke to Joe. "I know what this dream is about. I've been thinking about changing jobs for six months but I've been afraid. I hate being an insurance adjuster. It's boring."

"Your dream sure tells you that you want more," said Joe. "You don't have to solve the job problem right now. Focus on the feeling. You really want to go off your rocker. It feels better to move and show yourself than be cautious and held back."

Joe talked to the whole group about Michael's experience: "Don't let techniques get in the way of just being with the person who tells you a dream. Techniques are just aids when the person is having trouble expressing something, as Michael did at the beginning of his dream. The Make-It-Work Technique we've been talking about today has six steps, but they don't always come in order.

"The first step is to just have the person tell his dream with as much feeling as he felt in the dream.

"The second step is to identify one important picture in the dream and ask, specifically, 'How do you feel in that picture?'

"The third step is to help the person create some other pictures which contrast with the one in the dream and ask, 'How do you feel in that picture?'

"The fourth step is to ask the person when he's had a feeling similar to the one pictured in his dream and have the person describe the real time just as he first described his dream.

"The fifth step is to help him locate what he left out, what didn't he do or say that he felt; and help him do it or say it now.

"The sixth step is to go back to the original dream picture and ask, 'What could I do now in this picture?'

"By the time you reach step six, if the person can go all the way like Michael did, you will shift the dream; often it will become a Breakthru Dream with more awareness, more feeling, more expression, and more activity."

The group was excited as Michael went on. He knew what

he wanted from his dreams—to be more than an old woman and that meant being a powerful man.

As the group continued, Joe had Michael sustain his excitement. By the time Joe stopped the session everyone was charged with energy.

Michael left and found Judy waiting despondently in their room. She had been thinking of asking Michael to leave the workshop so that they could go home. As she sank lower with her runaway thoughts, Michael filled the doorway.

He shouted, "Judy, I'm a liar. I'm a liar. I've been lying to you, and me, and my boss for too long. You know when I'm acting down and out and unclear, I'm an old lady in a rocking chair. I want to live from what I really know. I want to change and grow. I'm through playing it safe. My dreams have been trying to pound that into me for months and months and now I am ready to stop being pounded and start living."

Judy was blown away. Mike's words were like a hurricane. She didn't expect him to breakthrough; she thought they would go back and continue living in their old way. "Michael, I don't know what to say."

"I do, I know, and I'm going to keep saying it."

At five the whole group met again for a question-and-answer session. Riggs was talking when Michael and Judy came in. "If you allow yourself to see and experience what the dream is showing you, then you allow the dream to move you, change you. The next morning you begin an outreach, however timid, to a friend, a mate—maybe even a stranger. There's satisfaction in living out the teachings of a Breakthru Dream that lasts."

Judy whispered to Michael, "That's what you're doing, Michael. You're really letting yourself change. I like you getting out of that rocker."

"Me too."

A man in the audience said, "I believe dreams are important and can tell me something but I still have trouble remembering them."

First Lee and then Joe answered him, "Many people have trouble just remembering their dreams; it means they have trouble remembering their feelings. Here is a simple test: At night try to remember what you had for breakfast, try to remember the setting and, if you were with someone, try to remember the conversation and your thoughts. People who can remember their dreams can also remember their waking life—they have a 'feel for it.' Those people who can't remember their dreaming can't remember details of their waking.

"But the way to remember is *not* to try to remember, but to communicate what you do remember. The first step toward making your dreams, or your life, work is to talk about what is going on with you. Making your dreams work is not a solitary project—don't go off and try to carve your dreams into shape like a solitary wood carver."

Joe went on, "Even if you talk about not remembering your dreams, that will be an important step toward making your dreams work. One of our patients complained about not being able to remember his dreams. So we asked him one of the same things we asked you at the beginning of the workshop: 'What did you have for breakfast?' He answered, 'Oh, just the usual.' 'What?' 'I'm not sure . . . juice and coffee and toast.' 'What kind of juice?' 'Orange juice.' 'What kind of toast?' 'Wheat toast.' 'Did you eat it dry?' 'Oh no. I put butter and jam on it.' 'What kind of jam?' 'Strawberry.' . . . and so on. Clearly this man did not communicate much. He generalized about his life, but did not share details about how he actually lives."

A young man asked, "Would you explain some more about how the Dream Maker Approach is different from the Interpretive Approach? I just can't seem to stop trying to figure out what my dreams mean."

Jerry answered, "You don't have to stop interpreting, just start doing something else first."

Riggs went on, "It is true that a dream does have a meaning and sometimes several meanings. However, *what a dream means is secondary to what a dream pictures.* The dream pictures are not formed to convey a message or meaning, as though they were in a forgotten language; they are formed as pictures of our feelings. They tell us immediately, without interpretation, what our feelings look like. They tell us directly how our bodies feel and how our lives feel.

"Asking what a dream means is like asking what a painting or a piece of music means. Very few paintings or symphonies are programmatic or verbal; they are expressive. *What they most mean is how you feel when you see them or hear them.*"

Joe said, "I want you to write down two basic steps:

"Number one is to *let yourself feel the dream.* Don't focus on what the dream means, but on how you feel in the dream.

"Number two is to *communicate your dream and how you feel* to someone close to you. Don't keep your dream feelings private and secret."

Lee explained, "The most important thing to do with your dreams in the morning is to *talk about them.* Start to bring your dreams into your life."

The leaders went on to answer more questions for about twenty-five minutes and then broke for dinner. Before leaving everyone was given a workshop handout and asked to read it before returning. Here is an extract from the handout:

## WORKSHOP HANDOUT—MAKING DREAMS WORK
**Moods**

It is amazing how people do not notice how affected they are by their dreams. Usually the people who are most blindly and helplessly affected are the very people who are "too busy to pay attention to meaningless things like dreams." Such people inevitably pay a high price for their ignorance. They are, literally, left to float all day in their own feelings. Dream feelings which are not specifically felt and brought into daily life become moods. People "get up on the wrong side of the bed" and never realize that they can influence whether or not they stay on "the wrong side."

There is a big difference between being moody and feeling something specific. Moods are diffuse feelings. When a mood gets pictured in a dream the dream usually does not have the dreamer in it at all. Everything is outside the dreamer. He sees pictures but he does not see himself. Sometimes he is not even aware of himself looking at pictures. He floats on pictures of his feelings (or submerges under his feelings) instead of having feelings inside himself and expressing and acting from those feelings.

A typical dream mood fragment would be something like this: Little children are picked up in a car pool. The car is crowded. Later the children sat at long tables in a huge basement.

The dreamer, a woman, does nothing but see the scene. She is not a participant in the scene and she is not even aware, during the dream, of herself doing the looking. There is a sense of vacancy and noninvolvement about the dream pictures. We can expect that, unless she talked about the dream after waking up, she probably went through the first part of her day with the same pervading mood.

Contrast the previous dream, which conveys pictures of a person living from moods, with this dream: "I am working for this lawyer who is a real nice person. I like working for him. I feel really powerful because I can just reach out and grab him by the arm and say, 'I need to talk to you.'"

There is a very different feeling about this dream—because the dreamer lives from his feelings differently than the first dreamer. In fact, this dreamer does pull people aside when he needs to talk. And he talks about everything in his life—his work, his dreams, his sex life, his play, everything.

**During the Day**

The power of feelings is that they can energize or drain you throughout the day. A person who has a bad dream cannot just get over it by talking once and then forgetting it. If he forgets the dream, he will still be affected during the day by the dream feelings.

Try to remember your dreams during the day. If you have already talked about them in the morning this will be easy to do. If you haven't, then it will be difficult.

The value of remembering dream images during the day is twofold. First, it will help you to avoid being unconsciously affected by the dream feelings. And second, you have a second chance to choose your feelings instead of your moods.

The immense value of dreams is that they picture our life without making it reasonable. Dreams make feeling sense, *always*, even if they do not make rational sense. This is why dreams can be our ally against a "pseudo-world" of reasonable images. It may "be sensible" not to say what we really feel to a boss or authority figure, but if our dream shows us crushed under a packload of canned goods, then it is showing us directly the consequences of such "reasonableness."

A very simple yet powerful thing to do during the day is to refer to the dream pictures of the night and picture how they would apply in the situation in which we are living. In that way we can *see* our feelings, either working for us or against us.

If they are working against us, we can then carry the picture one step further and imagine how the dream might change for the better. For example, the woman who dreamt of little children in the car pool could imagine, "I see myself as one of those children. I don't want to stay in the basement. I start yelling, 'Let me out of here.' " Of course, such an imaginative picturing of how things could be would have consequences for her life. She will have a choice: to live anonymously like the child she was, or to live like the adult she wants to be.

## What to Do at Night

It may seem peculiar to give you advice about what to do when you are dreaming. "How can I remember what to do when I'm dreaming? Dreaming is dreaming. I'm not awake to remember."

But the fact is you can remember, in a feeling sense, what to do in your dreams just as well as you can remember what to do when awake. We are not talking about tricks and gimmicks; we don't mean we are going to teach you to be a dream wizard in the way people try to become memory wizards.

What you can become is a feeling person, someone in touch with feelings. Since dream feelings and waking feelings are essentially no different, you can do at night with your feelings just what you do during the day.

## It Is Possible to Try Something Different

Here is what you can do at night in your dreams (and during the day in your waking life):

One. *Feel everything that happens to you no matter how bad it seems.* Your feelings, when felt, cannot destroy you. It is only the twisting and hiding of feelings that destroys.

Two. *Get help from your friends.* There is no reason you should dream alone any more than you should live alone. Bring your friends into your dreams. Talk to them in your dreams just as you do in your waking life.

Three. *Do more than you think is possible.* There is no reason you should limit yourself in your dreams, just as there is no reason you should limit your feelings in waking life.

Notice how different those instructions are from the way you ordinarily think about your dreams. You can immediately, tonight, start to do what we suggest. After all, the Dream Maker Approach to dreaming is no harder to learn than the passive approach you learned as a child or the interpretive approach you learned as an adult.

TRY THIS: Go back over this chapter and pick out the parts that affected you the most. Those are the parts which have something to say to you right now about your dreams and your life. Now do this: Imagine yourself at the workshop with Michael and Judy and the group leaders. Imagine that you are talking to one of the leaders, Joe or Jerry or Riggs or Lee. What would you tell them about your dreams? What would you ask them? Carry on a short imaginary conversation and see if it changes your approach to your dreams and feelings.

# 14
# New Kinds of Dreams

That evening Michael and Judy had dinner with several other people they had met at the workshop. Judy surprised herself by talking even more than Michael; usually she would hang back a little when they were in groups, especially with strangers. Michael had not heard Judy talk that way before; he looked at her with a new appreciation.

After dinner Judy stayed on in the dining room to talk to her new friend Alice. Judy told her what had happened to her that afternoon, how she had wanted to run away, how she had wanted to try and protect a little piece of her life.

Alice was learning well at the workshop, "Do you think that it has anything to do with Michael?"

"No, not really. I think I am afraid of something happening to me. It's like I make up reasons to collapse."

They looked at each other and smiled. They had surprised themselves by talking so freely and directly; they both felt smarter.

It was getting close to the time for the evening session when Judy found Michael in their room. She thought of waiting but she didn't. "Mike, I've got something to admit to you. I haven't been very much of my own woman here. I thought you were getting tired and angry, so I was getting ready to talk you into leaving. I know that all sounds complicated but that's what was happening. When you came in and told me all that stuff I was shocked. I felt like I was caught with my hand in the cookie jar."

Michael wrapped his arms around her. "Judy, how many times do we make it just by the skin of our teeth? We're good for each other. Let's go find out some more. You know I realized these guys will be leaving tomorrow."

Judy and Michael sat close together in the big meeting room. All four of the leaders were there. Joe was talking: "One of the most dangerous and misleading things anyone can do with their dreams is try to control them. For most people, growing up is synonymous with control. An adult is supposed to be someone who is in control, of himself or herself, of the situation. That's a fraud!"

Michael whispered to Judy, "You know I feel like I'm really growing up. I like the feeling."

Judy whispered back, "Me too."

"Actually very few people ever really grow up," Joe continued, "they just get bigger and older. Real growing up could mean becoming more and more capable of both sensing the world and expressing yourself in the world. Normal people do acquire the ability to know and control parts of the world and control themselves, but they have very little capacity for expression. It's not unusual to see someone with an intelligence quotient of 150 and an emotional quotient of 25. We even have popular stereotypes for people, such as 'absent-minded professor' who can think but can't talk or touch or play."

A man at the side of the room said, "For a period in my life, about two months, I was afraid to dream at all. Every dream I had seemed like a nightmare."

Joe answered him, "Dreaming is friendly. Even when you have a nightmare and feel terrible, the Dream Maker Process is simply picturing the way your body feels."

A woman near the front responded, "I tried for six months to control my dreams so I could fly. Sometimes I actually did it, but after a while it didn't seem to affect me much more than taking a plane to New York."

Lee told her, "When we describe the different types of dreams, like flying dreams, we don't intend that you try then to have your dreams be like the dreams we mention. There is no dream better than whatever dream you are having. Your dreams show your life. Until you feel your life, you cannot change it from the inside. There is no super technology of dreaming.

"We do not want to undertake yet another effort at self-improvement. Your self, your feelings, need no improvement. They simply need attention and tender loving care."

After this introduction the leaders opened the meeting up to more questions and answers about different types of dreams.

Judy asked, "You talk sometimes about Great Dreams, but I'm not sure I know what you mean. I don't know for sure if I've had one."

Jerry answered her, "A Great Dream is what a dream can be. In a complete Breakthru Dream there is full awareness, full feeling, full expression, and full activity. We call such a dream a Great Dream. Other kinds of dreams usually just have one of those features but a Great Dream has them all. It shows you what your dreams can be and what your life can be. . . . But don't try to have Great Dreams. Take the dreams you have and feel them and then feel how you can make them work for you by increasing your awareness, your feeling level, and your expressiveness. Every dream contains the possibilities for a Great Dream—if you will let those possibilities come through.

"We will explain three types of Breakthru Dreams which are important, but often misunderstood. Power Dreams, Clear Dreams, and Bright Dreams. Each of these dream types can be understood for what it is (and what it isn't) when related to the Great Dream. Each is a kind of Breakthru Dream."

Riggs continued, "In fact, there is *no* limit on dreams. Dream reality does not have the same time-space limits as waking reality. When we are faced with an obstacle in our dreams there is *no reason* why we shouldn't fly over it or burst through it."

Joe elaborated by telling one of his dreams. "The most significant Power Breakthrus are those which are also Great Dreams; those dreams in which the dreamer is not only extraordinarily powerful but also fully feeling and active and expressive. Here is a sample Great Dream:

*I am with Riggs outside an old house. I have a strange feeling about something, I don't know what. Then, near the house, I see a glow envelop a bush. At first I'm afraid and want just to get away. Then I go into it instead of away from it. I feel surrounded and then infused by white light power. Afterwards I feel whole, complete, sure. I say to Riggs, "The light is my feeling, it's inside of me, if I move with my feelings." Later the light comes into the house and I take it into me again and again, and I feel whole and complete and sure.*

"The significance of this dream is that the dreamer feels the power at first outside of him and then inside of him. He moves toward what he fears and assimilates the power of his own feelings. In some ways this dream is both a Power Dream and a Bright Dream."

A young man near the rear of the audience said, "I'm not sure I fully see the difference between Power Dreams and Bright Dreams. Could you explain it a little more?"

Lee cautioned him, "Remember that the categories we are using are just words about experiences. It is more important to have the experience and live it through than to categorize it. Don't try to decide if a dream is 80% Power and 20% Bright. Simply use these categories to understand the basic feelings within your dreams.

"The basic difference between a Power Dream and a Bright Dream is that the Power Dream *follows* an expressive shift in waking and a Bright Dream precedes or signals the possibility of such a shift."

Jerry gave an example, "Here is a sample Bright Dream:

*I landed on the moon. Everything there was exceptionally beautiful, luminous and sharp. I could see the crystal black sky, the beautiful landscape and the strange lighting; it was beautiful, all beautiful.*

"Notice that the dream is literally bright or luminous—the pictures have glow to them that seems unearthly.

"What Bright Dreams signify about feelings is the need and possibility that the dreamer shift to an expanded feeling level. What the dream does is picture something beyond the world you usually live in. They say, 'Here is another world.' But the dream pictures are not really showing you another world outside of you; they are representing another world inside of you. The Bright Dream is picturing a more intense feeling condition. You can actually see the glow or intensity of it.

"The Bright Dream pictures the increase in your feeling level; you're beginning to glow with feeling.

"But if you have one of these Bright Dreams and don't actually shift your feeling level, it will have been of no importance. It just signifies another opportunity missed."

Next, Lee said, "Now before we tell you about Clear Dreams I want you to be clear right here and now. Are you aware of how you feel? Are you aware that you are feeling anything? Could you express how you feel to someone next to you? Try it."

For the next few seconds the room was filled with a low murmur as each person told the person next to him what he could clearly feel was happening.

Joe elaborated, "One kind of Clear Dream is a dream in which you are aware during the dream that you are dreaming. These are very important dreams. And they, like Bright Dreams and Power Dreams, become most important when they are extended to become Great Dreams. So, if you are aware that you are dreaming, and you are aware enough to tell yourself to do something that's expressive or to stop doing something that's defensive, you tell yourself, 'I can choose,' and that can be a Great Dream. They are not common."

Then Riggs, "A Clear Dream reveals a feeling process

which is different from repression. In a Clear Dream we are aware that we are alive and dreaming. We are aware that we are creating the pictures. This kind of awareness is as rare in waking as in dreaming."

A man asked, "Why is it so rare?"

Jerry gave him a detailed answer. "Clear Dreams, Power Dreams, and Bright Dreams are all Breakthru Dreams. They all represent an ascendence of the Dream Maker force over the counterforces of repression. When there is a full breakthrough, so that a dreamer is fully expressive, fully active, and fully aware, we call that a Great Dream."

Riggs then picked up on the explanation. "What is common to all dreams whatever type they are is that they are attempts to complete feelings and return you to a balance between your feelings about something and your expression of those feelings."

A young woman toward the front asked, "Are Breakthru Dreams the best dreams to have?"

Joe answered, *"The best dream to have is the one you are having.* Your dreams, even if symbolic and mixed-up and passive, represent the best effort you can make to express your feelings. If you pay attention to the way you are, then the Dream Maker within you can start to show you what your life is and what it could be."


At 8:30 P.M. people again divided into smaller groups. This time the groups did not work with dreams at all. Instead the group leaders asked each person to describe a real life scene, something that had happened to them recently, and to describe the happening as though it were a dream.

Judy's group was again led by Riggs. After most people in the group had described scenes from their lives, he commented: "Do you see how each person's life picture is exactly like his dream picture? Each has the same amount of feeling, the same amount of expression, the same amount of activity and awareness."

Judy spoke to Riggs and the people in the group. "You know, I feel different since I've been here. I'm taking it easier. I want to keep feeling this way. I even took a nap this afternoon and had a little dream that was just perfect for me."

Riggs said, "Tell us, Judy."

"All I remember now is the last part. I'm running downhill. It's easy for me. I think to myself, 'This is the way I want to live—it's easy for me.' Then I woke up, but I had the same good feeling I had in the dream."

Riggs spoke directly to her, "If you live out the consequences of that one dream picture, it will change your entire life. That one picture shows you a whole new way to live your life."

Judy could hear what Riggs was saying. She felt his words meet her feelings: "The process of a dream is the feeling movement, toward or away from expression. The content of a dream is the story or subject."

Judy's group was over about 9:00 P.M. Everyone lingered, talking and enjoying themselves. By listening to each other's dreams, they had made a deeper contact, a contact that made their relationships seem much older than a single day.

Michael's evening group was being led by Jerry who told everyone that they would take steps, little steps that lead to big changes. He asked people to tell a dream they had experienced within the last week that bothered them. Michael related this dream:

*I dreamt that Judy was sitting on a pedestal. I could see her above me. I felt little. Then, I remembered to touch myself, to feel myself—I began to do this. The more that I did, the larger I became. As I grew, my cock began to get larger and larger. I was soon very large. I was as high as Judy was. I felt very glad. I wanted to fuck her. I took her into my arms, she felt small at first, but the more we touched the bigger she became. Then we were laying on soft grass having wonderful sex. We were laughing and talking very intimately. I knew I loved her very deeply.*

Michael said, "What should I do?"

Jerry didn't answer directly, he asked a question, "What is it, Michael? What do you want to know about this dream?"

Michael was white with fear. "Well, how do I begin?"

Then in a very sly voice Jerry said, "Miiiichaellll . . . are you afraid of having too much feeling?"

"No."

"Then why don't you try doing what this dream is telling you."

"What's that?"

"You know, Mike, I was talking with Joe this afternoon and he told me you might try to get back into the rocking chair. I think that is what is happening."

Michael smiled, "I know what to do. I love having that much feeling with Judy. I really like it when I get turned on and don't have any thoughts. In that dream my cock was so big I didn't have time for anything but sex with Judy."

Jerry was laughing, "What do you think Sigmund Freud would have to say about that?"

The group was laughing. It was obvious that the dream was working for Michael.

He stood up and said, "I am out of the rocking chair, there is no room in it for me and Judy, and I want her, I want her, I want her."

Everyone was roaring with laughter.

As the group got louder Don decided to break it all up. "What about me, what about the average guy on the street? How do I even get to remember dreams? When do I become a Dream Maker?"

Jerry answered firmly, "Each night everyone comes very close to becoming a Dream Maker. Many people already have had dreams that, if lived out, would have helped them become a

Dream Maker. What we have taught you is that to become a Dream Maker you must be willing to live from what you dream. To make dreams work for you rather than against you, you must come out of the shadows."

Don snapped back at Jerry, "Well I don't dream."

Jerry turned toward him and bore down, "Do you ever have fantasies?"

Don answered, "Yes."

"Do you ever have hateful thoughts?"

"Yes."

"Loving thoughts?"

"Yes."

"Do you feel special?"

"Sometimes," Don said guardedly.

"Do you feel worse than other people?"

"Yes."

"Do you ever get bored with the games you play?"

"Sure."

"Then you already had a chance to be a Dream Maker."

Don answered back, "Yeh, but I don't have any big dreams like you guys talk about."

Jerry smiled. "You won't ever have them unless you learn to allow the Dream Maker some more room."

"What do you mean?"

"Well, in every question I asked you, there is really a second question, a roominess question: Do you talk as much as you think?"

Don was stopped in his tracks. He tried an old ploy. "I came here to find out about dreams—not to talk about thoughts and fantasies. I don't think you know what you are talking about."

Jerry's smile was gone. "It seems to me that you want to make everything outside of you your own dream. What about the way you are trembling, right now? Do you want to find out about that, or do you want to follow that program you have concocted in your head?"

Don heard Jerry. He knew what he was talking about, "I didn't know that I was trembling. I would like you to help me."

The Dream Maker had been in the room since the beginning. He had been waiting for this man. He was having a waking dream—it did not matter what he was saying, what mattered was that he was doing something, saying something; he was showing his feelings.

Jerry asked Don if he would like to go deeper, if he would like to experience more of his own Dream Maker. Don said he was scared. But, also, that he wanted something more. As the man spoke with Jerry, the Dream Maker came again. Jerry told him to allow the shaking; the more Don allowed the shaking, the more the Dream Maker became visible. Don had been trapped in a role all of his life and now that role was being shaken. The Dream Maker brought tears to his eyes. Don stood there, a stranger to Jerry, and yet it was as if they knew each other in some primitive way. Don's face was full of color; his faded and deep-set eyes began to glisten.

Don began speaking with a deeper voice. "I have been sitting in this room with you for hours, realizing that you would leave this room, this town, and probably never come back. I wanted to say something to you; I don't know what. Just that I am here; I hear what you are saying. I want you to know me even if it is for these few hours. Sometimes I'll say anything just to get started."

He talked to the rest of the group for over half an hour. He talked and talked. His first step was realizing that he was dreaming during the day; once he began to know that, then he could remember his dreams.


After the evening groups, everyone met together again in the large meeting room at 9:30 P.M. All of the group leaders were there and all of the workshop participants. The voices in the room were a little subdued because many people were already feeling sad at saying good-bye to new friends.

The leaders had everyone think over the dreams they had been working with and come up with a single Dream Maker word to express the teaching from their own dream.

Jerry said, "This word is just yours. It's from you and for you. Hear yourself say it. Feel the word in your body as you say it."

Michael heard himself saying, "Touch . . . TOUCH . . . TOUCH . . . TOUCH . . ." He could feel the excitement of that word for his life.

Judy was saying, "Easy, easy, easy . . ." She felt relaxed, her voice sounded soft to her like a caress.

All around them people were saying their own Dream Maker words. Some were loud, shouting; others quiet. The whole room was full of sound.

Later the leaders talked about community: "We hope you will carry over much of what has happened to you into your lives wherever you live. Those of you who live in the same city could think about getting together regularly for a dream group. People who want to stay in touch with us about their dreams are welcome to join the Dream Maker Associate Program where you can write regularly to a group leader and share your dreams.

"We have explained how important it is to communicate your dreams. To do that, all you need is someone who will listen and share his own dreams. Going deeper into dreams requires that you have several people as you make the move from just talking about your feelings to expressing, actually sharing and living your feelings."

Michael wondered to himself if he would be able to share dreams with others. He knew he'd need help from Judy.

Judy felt good about what she and Michael had been learning. She was really starting to value her dreams.

The speakers went on, "There are a great many educated people who are emotionally retarded. They can't talk from their feelings; they can't reach out and make contact with other people; and they can't express their feelings with complete crying or laughing or shouting or moving."

Judy was beginning to feel very clear about how she wanted to live, and dream. She also felt sure that she and Michael could do much more sharing of their dreams.

"The value of dream groups goes beyond sharing dreams. By sharing dreams people share feelings. You can begin to share both dream feelings and waking feelings. Such sharing takes time because it goes against our main cultural tradition. Some of the early American Indian groups, like the Iroquois, had a tradition of dream sharing which was much more sophisticated than our own verbal, cognitive, what-does-it-mean tradition. Also there is a Malaysian group called the Senoi which has a sophisticated dream culture. You will have to create your own—we hope this workshop has helped you get started."

With these last words the workshop ended.


## Life-Style, Life Time and Life Span

The Dream Maker workshop we have described lasted just one day, but for some of the people who were there its influence will continue for years. Certainly both Judy and Michael made a number of changes in their lives from what they had learned to do with their dreams. We believe the main value of these workshops is not so much in what happens during the one day, although a lot does happen, but in the continuing influence the Dream Maker can have on the life of anyone who learns to respond to his dreams.

In the workshops we do not try to give the participants something to imitate; instead we put them in touch with what they already have—their own Dream Maker.

It is easy to show someone a life-style; advertisements bombard us every day with pictures of "the good life," or "the natural man," or "the beautiful woman." We all grow up learning about how we should look. The trouble with all these pictures is that they have no feeling.

Because most people grow up without real feeling contact they do not grow up inside. All that happens is that their bodies grow up and their costumes change and their roles become more sophisticated. As people learn a life-style, they give up their life time.

This condition of style over life shows up in dreams. The Dream Maker exists in our lifetime; again and again the Dream Maker shows us pictures of our life. When we shift from living a style to living from feeling, our dream pictures transform, we begin to have Breakthru Dreams.

We have shown Breakthru Dreams in which dreamers clearly shift from the way they were in their past to the way they can be in their present. Such a shift is only achieved by people who feel their past. Most people flee their past and try to fashion a life-style different from that of their mother and father. But inside, in their feelings, they remain children.

There is a popular saying that "those who cannot remember the past are condemned to repeat it." Nowhere is this saying more true than in dreams. Everyone has a Dream Maker who can create new dreams. But dreams are not advertisements; you cannot buy a lifetime of feeling, nor can you imitate a Dream Maker.

People who live styles have little sense of life or death. Anyone who begins to sense his life span will feel both the preciousness of his life time and the real limits of his life span. There is not enough time for everything; we must choose. A person living from his feelings chooses from inside himself; what he chooses now relates to what he has chosen before and what he wants for his future. The person lost in a life-style hardly chooses at all. His style chooses for him: "do this," "do that," "say this," "don't say that," "talk to him," "don't talk to her." All he knows is what fits the style; he does not know what feels good to him.

Our Dream Maker never gives up. We keep being told by our dreams how our life feels, but we can't be made to choose life time over life-style. Everyone has the choice, but not everyone chooses.

# 15
# After the Workshop

Both Michael and Judy did make some important choices for themselves in the months following the workshop. Michael got a new job, as an executive trainee in a large travel agency.

Judy and Michael began to talk a lot more closely and intensely to their friends. Mostly, Judy and Michael didn't talk about some new theory; they just talked. There was a growing tenderness between them. They didn't want to go to as many shows or as many parties and they both thought that even work took too much of their time away. They began to hoard what was precious, time, even at the expense of their friends' company.

It would have been incongruous for Michael's friends to say, "Hey, look, Michael and Judy are becoming Dream Makers." But it wouldn't have been really too odd if someone had said, "Something is happening."

Michael and Judy wanted to take care of and learn more about themselves. They talked to each other, and often were more confused than they had ever been. Then for moments or hours or even days at a time they would become perfectly clear; they would know what to do and where they were going.

These days they came to call their "special days." In many ways that is what the Dream Maker is about—helping people find what is special for them. For Michael and Judy it meant that they cried more, they fought more, but they had a new motto when they fought—"no winners, no losers and no quitters—only lovers."

One morning, Michael got up very quietly; he put the coffee on and heated two cinnamon rolls he had bought at Judy's favorite bakery. He put a single candle on one of them.

Once everything was in place he bent over and kissed his lover, "Good morning, honey. Happy birthday."

It was six o'clock, but Judy woke up quickly. She felt full. She knew that this was her time, from her lover, and this was her life. The Dream Maker had done what it does best—make changes.

The next morning Judy had a Great Dream. This is what she wrote in her dream book:

In the week before this particular dream I had been feeling good but muddy. I was pushing; I was working hard, trying to stay alive inside but I sounded like a robot when I look back at my diary about that time, e.g., "Tomorrow I want to a) go visit Alice, b) start eating bran, c) go jogging, etc.

I went to sleep and for the first time became aware of someone talking to me in my dreams. I had been wandering around a mansion for some time—filled with statues and other art treasures, vases, goblets, pictures, and ornate furniture. I must have been in a fog because the first thing I can remember besides a haze of pictures and artwork was someone standing next to me saying, "They aren't really statues, you know, they're really people locked up inside." I said, "Oh, no, no they're not." And the person replied, "Yes, they are. Look, look closely." I remember squinting my eyes and looking deeper into the art treasures—trying to see inside them. I began to see a little face locked away into a beautiful, ornate goblet. Then I noticed a face carved into a wooden carved mirror frame. The voice said, "Here, take some of this potion, it's magic solution—you'll see." So I took some of the water in my hands and threw it at one statue near me. The statue began to unstiffen and unbend and stepped off its base. I was amazed. I threw some more potion on a picture and a lady slowly stepped out of the picture. I was more amazed. I became almost frenzied. I ran around the mansion flinging water at the pictures and statues. When I realized that there *really were* people locked up inside, I wanted them OUT! And *fast*. I was off unlocking more people when I heard the original statue and lady that I had unlocked moaning and groaning. Their joints were stiff and aching; they had trouble moving their knees and legs. They were afraid, I heard them saying, "We didn't want to be unlocked. We were happy there. What will we do? What will we do now? We don't know what to do. What will we do all day? When we were locked up we spent the day in the picture or standing up on our pedestals. What'll we do now?" I was utterly stupefied that they would say such a thing—dumbfounded and disappointed. "What are you talking about?" I shouted. "Don't you understand? You're free now. You can go any place now. You can do anything you want to do. You're free now. *Wake up. Wake up. Wake up!*"

Judy is still living out the consequences of that dream. It may take her years to grow into the life her dream showed.

Both Judy and Michael began to talk with their friends not just about wines and restaurants and movies but about their lives and how they felt and what they wanted and the difficulties they had; they were being real friends.

When we returned to Chicago six months later to give an advanced Dream Maker workshop for the people who had attended the first one, we found that so many friends of the first group of people also wanted to attend that we organized another introductory workshop. Chicago was becoming a Dream Maker outpost.

This story of Michael and Judy cannot be concluded with a safe and happy ending like "They all lived together without problems under the guidance of the Dream Maker." The Dream Maker does not solve all the problems of living. It simply gives people who follow the Dream Maker Approach a different way of relating to their lives.

The Dream Maker Approach to problems is like the gardener's; a problem is often just a seed and you cannot always tell the seed weeds from seed plants. In fact some weeds are curative. The Dream Maker Approach is a way for people to feel what makes their life grow.

# APPENDIXES: WHAT MORE YOU CAN DO

# A
## Information about
## The Center Foundation
## and The Center for
## Feeling Therapy

### The Dream Capabilities Assessment Test

The first kind of "something more" we want to encourage every-one to do is to take the Dream Capabilities Assessment Test (DCAT) which was developed from our long-range research program on dreams. You can send a copy of the test reproduced in chapter 13 on pages 148–156 or obtain a new test by writing to:

Lee Woldenberg, M.D.
Director, Dream CAT Project
The Center Foundation
7165 Sunset Blvd.
Los Angeles, California 90028

or by telephoning:

(213) 874-3136

In sending the Dream test, please include the following informa-tion:

NAME: _____

ADDRESS: _____
             Street                City           State       Zip

PHONE: HOME_____WORK _____

AGE___SEX___SINGLE___MARRIED___DIV. ___CHILDREN___

EDUCATION: _____ OCCUPATION: _____

INCOME: $0–6,000___ $6,000–12,000___ $12,000–20,000___
$20,000+ ___

How did you hear about this test? (Be specific.) _____
                                        (Radio, TV show,
                                       newspaper, friend,
                                       etc.)

I would like further information about dreams:   Yes___ No___

I hereby release all materials submitted by me to The Center Foundation for use in its Research Program. The information obtained on this test is strictly confidential and will be used solely by The Center Foundation.

_____
Signature

    The test will immediately be sent to you. It takes less than fifteen minutes to complete. When you return the test it will be scored and you will receive a summary profile about your level of dream functioning and your potentialities. (Also, be sure to enclose a stamped, self-addressed envelope.) There is no charge to you for the test and no charge for the test scoring. By taking the test you will give us information that we can add to our nationwide survey of dream capabilities and we will give you information about your own dream characteristics.

## The Center Foundation

    The Center Foundation which sponsors the test research and other dream investigations is a nonprofit research, service, and educational organization. The Foundation sponsors research on psychotherapy, dreams, and sleep; it also offers a variety of educational and training programs, and is the administrative arm of the Dream Maker

Program. The Foundation employs both professionals and paraprofessionals; it is administered by a board of directors, all of whom are psychotherapists.

There are three classes of membership in the Foundation open to the public. A *subscribing member* receives a bimonthly Center newsletter about the lectures, workshops, publications, and tapes which are offered by the Foundation. This membership is open to anyone who would like to regularly receive information about the Dream Maker Approach, Feeling Therapy, and applications of Feeling Therapy. *Associate memberships* are open to all interested persons who sign up for one of the correspondence educational programs offered by the Foundation. These educational programs do not offer psychotherapy but are designed to teach people how to apply some of the insights and practices of Feeling Therapy to their everyday lives. Programs are available in a number of subject areas, including a Dream Maker Associate Program (for more information about this program see Appendix B). *Supporting members* of the Foundation are individuals who have donated sums of money to support various service or research programs.

Some of the projects the Foundation is now supporting include research on the psychophysiological correlates of psychotherapy, a documentary film series about Feeling Therapy, and the preparation of an audio and videotape library. All of these projects and others are supported by private donations, grants, and training fees.

The Foundation also sponsors the publication of a Dream Research newsletter to circulate information about current dream research findings and investigations among scientists specializing in this area of research. Any postgraduate professional or graduate student who would like to be included on the newsletter mailing list and who would like to submit information about their own research should write to:

Werner Karle, Ph.D.
Director of Research
The Center Foundation
7165 Sunset Blvd.
Los Angeles, California 90028

The Center Foundation is listed in the growth center list of the Association for Humanistic Psychology. We frequently send lecturers and workshop leaders to growth centers and universities throughout the United States and Canada. Information about these activities can be obtained by writing to The Center Foundation. (For more specific information about lectures concerning the Dream Maker Approach see Appendix B.)

## The Center for Feeling Therapy

Our other organization which offers programs connected with dreams is The Center for Feeling Therapy, Psychological Corporation. This Center is a multidisciplinary clinic, registered with the State of California Board of Medical Examiners as a psychological corporation.

The clinic was founded in 1971 to offer individual and group psychotherapy within the Feeling Therapy orientation. All the therapists at the Center are licensed professionals.

Feeling Therapy is one particular form of therapy within what is called the Functional School of Psychotherapy. Functional therapies blend together both of the major historical trends within modern clinical psychology: the Analytic-Experiential and the Behavior-Modification. For more information about the Functional Orientation as it relates to dreams consult *The Transformation of Dreams* or write for a listing of journal articles from The Center Foundation.

Because the clinic does only long-term therapy, we require that all prospective patients submit an autobiography and take a number of psychological tests. The information we obtain helps us to select only those patients who will benefit most from the therapy.

The clinic offers programs of both short-term intensive therapy (one month) for patients who will continue their therapy elsewhere and long-term intensive therapy (twelve plus months) for patients who can stay in the Los Angeles area.

All inquiries about applying for the therapy should be sent to the:

Applications Secretary
The Center for Feeling Therapy
7165 Sunset Blvd.
Los Angeles, California 90028

Telephone: (213) 874-3136

Due to the growing popularity of the Dream Maker programs and Feeling Therapy and the increasing professional recognition given the Functional Orientation, a number of individuals and organizations have adopted our names. Some of these organizations advertise in magazines and newspapers. We want to state emphatically that these so-called feeling therapies are not endorsed by us. The therapies they practice are very different from the one we describe in this book. We maintain a referral roster of professionals at The Center for Feeling Therapy in Los Angeles. Anyone who wants information about professionals and paraprofessionals who have been trained by us in one of our certificate programs can write to the Center.

# B
# Information about
# a Variety of
# Dream Maker Programs

Any person who has worked their way through the exercises in the twenty-one-day program of this book has already begun to learn to use his or her dreams more effectively. We will briefly describe a number of follow-up advanced programs that are available. To obtain detailed information about any one of these programs write to The Center Foundation. The board of directors of the Foundation is very concerned with affective education and to that end sponsors a variety of programs to help people become educated to their dreams and feelings. These programs range from very simple, short, low-cost programs for the general public to long-range ones for the education of mental health professionals. (The term "Dream Maker," as used in conjunction with Lectures, Associate Programs, Workshops, and Group Training programs, is a service mark of The Center Foundation.)

## Dream Maker Lectures

Therapists and researchers from The Center for Feeling Therapy and The Center Foundation travel all over the world to lecture about our dream research findings and ideas. We also offer an introductory lecture titled "Going Sane and the Breakthru Dream" which introduces nonprofessionals to the Dream Maker Approach. If you are interested in hearing a lecture on this topic in your city contact:

Dominic Cirincione
Administrative Director
The Center Foundation

7165 Sunset Blvd.
Los Angeles, California 90028

Telephone: (213) 874-3136

## The Dream Maker Associate Program

The two most influential psychologists of modern times, Sigmund Freud and Carl Jung, read and studied and wrote about their dreams throughout their lives.

The discoveries and thoughts and ideas of these two men formed the foundation for a great part of modern psychology. A private part of their lives which greatly influenced them was their mutual correspondence. Sigmund Freud and Carl Jung regularly wrote to each other about their dreams, their problems, and their lives.

The Dream Maker Associate Program is a special kind of correspondence program for you about your dreams, your feelings, your problems, and your life.

How does it work? The Dream Maker Associate Program is about you. In an individually designed program of affective education, your personal counselor will work with you to help you make your dream processes and feelings work for you.

You correspond with your individual counselor about your dream processes and feelings. There are three steps to the process of affective education:

1. Problem solving: Choosing a specific area, i.e., relationships, sex, overweight, anxiety, sleep, work, etc.

2. Expansion: Changing your dreams and expanding your feeling level.

3. Integration and transformation: Learning to incorporate your new level of dreaming and feeling into your life.

It's a step-by-step process. The goal is real sustained change. The way that kind of change takes place is through affective education with a personal counselor. Each time you and your counselor correspond you will receive a new teaching that will affect your dreams and expand and deepen your feeling level. The correspondence between you and your counselor will be the key to your transformation.

You learn . . . and then you experience . . . and then you change.

Write for more information and an application to:

Michele Callahan, M.A.
Director of the Dream Maker Associate Program
The Center Foundation
7165 Sunset Blvd.
Los Angeles, California 90028

## Dream Maker Workshops

We schedule one-day Dream Maker workshops and seminars in major cities throughout the world. The Dream Maker workshop will:

1. Introduce you to the most powerful psychological self-help tool there is—your own dreams.

2. Teach you about the discovery, theory, and practice of Breakthru Dreaming.

3. Test and evaluate your level of dream functioning on the Advanced Dream Capabilities Assessment Test.

4. In individual and group sessions, teach you to use your dreams for their natural function—as psychologically curative tools.

5. Show you how to have Breakthru Dreams that affect your life and the lives of people around you.

To learn more about attending a Dream Maker workshop in your area write to:

Jerry Binder, Ph.D.
Workshop Coordinator
The Center Foundation
7165 Sunset Blvd.
Los Angeles, California 90028

Telephone: (213) 874-3136

## Dream Maker Group Training

Group Training is an intensive program of teaching and guidance in transformative dreaming for groups of professionals and special groups of lay people. It is for *groups* of people who want to learn to help each other dream and live and work together with full feeling. Dream Group Training includes:

1. Experiential and didactic learning at a site in your home city, or at The Center Foundation's training facility in Los Angeles.

2. Follow-up individual and group sessions that continue to teach the theory and technique of transformative dreaming.

3. Practical instruction in using your dreams as powerful tools of transformation for your group.

Dream Group Training is a national and international program of limited enrollment for professionals and special groups of lay people. For information write to:

Richard Corriere, Ph.D.
Director of Training
The Center Foundation
7165 Sunset Blvd.
Los Angeles, California 90028

Telephone: (213) 874-3136

Finally, we invite everyone who reads this book and has questions about what we have said (or what we haven't said) to write to us. We will try to answer your questions and we would like to learn about your experiences with the Dream Maker Approach.

# REFERENCES &
# RECOMMENDED READING
# INDEX

# References and Recommended Reading

We list in these pages some recommended books that correspond to the four parts of *The Dream Makers*. For some listings we have supplied a few comments to tell you how the cited work relates to the Dream Maker Approach. The books, articles, and chapters marked with an asterisk (*) are used, mentioned, or quoted in *The Dream Makers*.

## Introduction and Part One: The Dream Maker Tradition

Corriere, R. "The Transformation of Dreams." Unpublished doctoral dissertation. University of California, Irvine, 1974. (This dissertation reports the original research on Transformative or Breakthru Dreaming. It contains an extensive literature review.)

Corriere, R.; Hart, J. T.; Karle, W.; Binder, J.; Gold, S.; Woldenberg, L. "Toward a New Theory of Dreaming," in *Journal of Clinical Psychology*, 1977, in press.

* Corriere, R.; Hart, J. T.; Woldenberg, L.; and Karle, W. *The Transformation of Dreams: A Functional Approach to Dreaming*, 1977, in press. (This forthcoming book reports on the research and clinical studies which developed into the Dream Maker Approach to dreams and dreaming. What we label "the Breakthru Dream" in *The Dream Makers* is called "the Transformative Dream" in *The Transformation of Dreams*. Readers who want more details, references, research, and theory should definitely consult this book.)

* Freud, S. *The Interpretation of Dreams*. (Eighth edition, revised) New York: Basic Books, 1960. (Anyone with a serious interest in the psychological theory of dreams should consult this book. In it Freud presented, in 1899, the foundations of his entire psychoanalytic theory. For a lengthy comparison of the Freudian Interpretive Approach with the Functional or Dream Maker Approach consult Corriere, Hart, et al. *The Transformation of Dreams*, 1977.)

Fromm, E. *The Forgotten Language*. New York: Grove Press, 1951. (Fromm's book is a popularization of the Interpretive Approach to dreams which calls for a decoding of the symbolism of censorship. Like Freud, Fromm has no recognition of a primary transformative (Dream Maker) process nor does he recognize the possibility of Transformative or Breakthru Dreams.)

* Hall, C. S., and van de Castle, R. L. *The Content Analysis of Dreams*. New York: Appleton-Century-Crofts, 1969. (This is the authoritative source book for information about the content of normal dreams. For a critique of Hall and van de Castle's approach see Corriere's *Transformation of Dreams*, 1974.)

* Hart, J.; Corriere, R.; and Binder, J. *Going Sane: An Introduction to Feeling Therapy*. New York: Aronson, 1975; New York: Delta, 1976. (*Going Sane* is a semipopular book addressed to both professionals and nonprofessionals. It describes the theory, techniques, and structure of Feeling Therapy and tells how the theory was developed.)

Karle, W.; Woldenberg, L.; and Hart, J. "Feeling Therapy," in V. Binder; A. Binder; and B. Rimland (eds.) *Modern Therapies*. New York: Prentice-Hall Spectrum Book, 1976. (This chapter provides a short introduction to Feeling Therapy.)

* Kroeber, T., and Heizer, R. F. *Almost Ancestors: The First Californians*. New York: Sierra Club-Ballantine Book, 1967. (This beautiful book contains photographs of Indians and many Indian songs, including the Wintu song we quoted in chapter 1.)

* Wallace, A. F. C. "Dreams and Wishes of the Soul," in *American Anthropologist*, 1958, LX 234–48. (This important article compares the Iroquois dream theory and practices with those of Freud. It tells of the Iroquois when they were at the peak of the dream-based culture in pre-Colonial times. It is from this source that we drew the guidelines for the fictionalized story of Tarachiwa.)

Wallace, A. F. C. *The Death and Rebirth of the Seneca*. New York: Vintage, 1969. (The anthropologist Wallace here tells of the late Colonial and early reservation history of one of the Iroquois tribes, the Seneca.)

For more reading related to the Dream Maker Tradition we recommend:

Brown, V., and Andrews, D. *The Pomo Indians of California and the Neighbors*. Healdsburg, California: Naturegraph, 1969.

Campbell, J. *The Hero with a Thousand Faces*. Cleveland: World Publishing, 1949.

———. *The Masks of God: Primitive Mythology*. New York: Viking Press, 1959.

———. *The Masks of God: Oriental Mythology*. New York: Viking Press, 1962.

———. *The Masks of God: Occidental Mythology.* New York: Viking Press, 1964.

———. *The Masks of God: Creative Mythology.* New York: Viking Press, 1968.

Castaneda, C. *Tales of Power.* New York: Simon and Schuster, 1974.

Coxhead, D., and Hiller, S. *Dreams: Visions of the Night.* New York: Avon, 1976.

Driver, H. E. *Indians of North America* (Second edition, revised). Chicago: University of Chicago Press, 1969.

Eliade, M. *Yoga: Immortality and Freedom* (Second edition). Princeton: Princeton University Press, 1968.

Lincoln, J. S. *The Dream in Primitive Cultures.* London: Cresset Press, 1935.

Middleton, J. (ed.). *Magic, Witchcraft and Curing.* Garden City, New York: Natural History Press, 1967.

Underhill, R. M. *Singing for Power.* Berkeley: University of California Press, 1968.

Von Grunebaum, G. E., and Callois, R. (eds.) *The Dream and Human Societies.* Berkeley: University of California Press, 1966.

## Part Two: Discovering the Dream Maker

The Senoi of Malaysia are a highly important culture of dreamers. They cultivate the Dream Maker Process to such an extent that Senoi dreams show a definite predominance of the Dream Maker Process over the Censoring Process. We recommend the following writings about the Senoi and applications of Senoi teachings:

Denton, R. K. *The Senoi: A Nonviolent People of Malaya.* New York: Holt, Rinehart and Winston, 1968.

Greenleaf, E. "Senoi Dream Groups," *Psychotherapy*, 1973, 10, 218–222.

Hart, J. T. "Dreams in the Classroom," *Experiment and Innovation*, 1971, 4, 51–66.

Noone, R., and Holman, D. *In Search of the Dream People.* New York: William Morrow, 1972.

Robertson, E. D. *Temiar Dream Songs from Malaya.* New York: Folkways Record and Text, Album P. 460, 1955.

* Stewart, K. "Magico-religious beliefs and practices in primitive society—a sociological interpretation of their therapeutic aspects." Unpublished doctoral dissertation, London School of Economics and Political Science, 1947.

————. "Mental Hygiene and World Peace," *Mental Hygiene*, 1954, XXXVIII, 387–403.

* ————. "Dream Theory in Malaya," in C. Tart (ed.) *Altered States of Consciousness.* New York: Wiley, 1969.

To read about the famous Freud-Jung controversy consult:

* Jung, C. G. *Memories, Dreams, Reflections.* New York: Vintage, 1961.

McGuire, W. (ed.). *The Freud/Jung Letters.* Princeton, N.J.: Princeton University Press, 1974.

One excellent source for Dakota dream songs and the songs of other American Indians is listed below:

* Curtis, N. (ed.). *The Indian's Book.* New York: Dover, 1950.

Also excellent for information about American Indians and Eskimos is:

* Rothenberg, J. (ed.). *Shaking the Pumpkin.* Garden City, New York: Doubleday & Co., 1972. (This book includes some poems by Nakasuk.)

One source for information about Siberian shamanistic rituals is:

* Eliade, M. *Shamanism: Archaic Techniques of Ecstasy.* Princeton, N.J.: Pantheon Books, 1964.

To read something about our own early explorations of transpersonal psychology read:

Hart, J. T. "The Zen of Hubert Benoit." *Journal of Transpersonal Psychology*, 1970, II, 141–167.

* ————. "Beyond Psychotherapy," in J. T. Hart and T. M. Tomlinson (eds.) *New Directions in Client-Centered Therapy.* Boston: Houghton Mifflin, 1970.

The last two sources drawn upon for this section of the book were:

* Hillman, J. *The Myth of Analysis.* Evanston, Illinois: Northwestern University Press, 1972.

* Meier, C. A. *Ancient Incubation and Modern Psychotherapy.* Evanston, Illinois: Northwestern University Press, 1967.

## Part Three: Twenty-one Days to Breakthru Dreaming— How to Make Your Dreams Work for You (and Not Against You)

All other current "how-to" programs that we know about focus on changing dream content or on interpreting dream symbols. We do not recommend such approaches. We do suggest that readers familiarize themselves with other modern theories of dreaming and some of the older traditional methods of dream work. Consult:

Altman, L. L. *The Dream in Psychoanalysis.* New York: International Universities Press, 1969.

Blofeld, J. *The Tantric Mysticism of Tibet.* New York: E. B. Dutton, 1970.

de Becker, R. *The Understanding of Dreams.* New York: Hawthorn Books, 1968.

Dement, W. C. *Some Must Watch While Some Must Sleep.* San Francisco: W. H. Freeman, 1972.

Evans-Wentz, W. Y. *The Tibetan Book of the Great Liberation.* New York: Oxford University Press, 1954.

Fingarette, H. *The Self in Transformation.* New York: Basic Books, 1903.

Freud, S. *On Dreams.* New York: W. W. Norton, 1952.

Govinda, L. A. *Foundations of Tibetan Mysticism.* London: Rider & Co., 1969.

Gutheil, E. A. *The Handbook of Dream Analysis* (second edition). New York: Washington Square Press, 1967.

Jung, C. G. *Man and His Symbols.* Garden City, New York: Doubleday, 1964.

McKenzie, N. *Dreams and Dreaming.* New York: Vanguard Press, 1965.

Mahoney, M. F. *The Meaning in Dreams and Dreaming.* New York: Citadel Press, 1966.

Milner, M. *On Not Being Able to Paint.* New York: International Universities Press, 1957.

Mookerjee, A. *Tantra Art.* New Delhi: Ravi Kummar, 1967.

Tucci, G. *The Theory and Practice of the Mandala.* London: Rider & Co., 1909.

## Part Four: Applying the Discovery—A Dream Maker Workshop

For more information about Dream Maker workshops consult Appendix B. To obtain articles about the workshops write to The Center Foundation in Los

Angeles. For reading about other kinds of workshops which use dreams we recommend:

Assagioli, R. *Psychosynthesis*. New York: Hobbs, Dorman and Company, 1965.

Perls, F. S. *Gestalt Therapy Verbatim*. Moab, Utah: Real People Press, 1969.

———. *In and Out of the Garbage Pail*. Moab, Utah: Real People Press, 1969.

Schutz, W. C. *Here Comes Everybody*. New York. Harper and Row, 1971.

# Index

Adler, Alfred, 37
adulthood, 70
Aesculaepius, 50
affective education, 88
Analytic-Experiential psychology, 192
Association for Humanistic Psychology, 191
awareness:
  alteration of, 2, 10, 31, 37, 90, 162, 172, 182
  in Clear Dream, 174-175
  of day-night links, 92
  exercise of, 91-92
  "go easy," 64
  of Reality, 31, 34

Baleh, 32-33, 34
Behavior-Modification psychology, 192
beliefs, questioning of, 105, 140
"Beyond Psychotherapy," 58
Binder, Jerry, see Jerry
Bob, 159-160
body:
  acceptance of, 71, 72-74
  awareness of, 92
  dreams of, 72-74, 171
body questions, in exercises, 93, 94, 95, 97
Boss, Medard, 37

Breakthru Dreams, 2, 10-11, 45, 54, 100, 124, 129, 136, 147, 182
  awareness shifted in, 2, 10, 31, 37, 162, 172, 182
  beginnings of, 23, 24, 50
  as Bright Dreams, 172, 173-174, 175
  characteristics of, 2, 10-12, 13, 146, 159
  children's, 61
  as Clear Dreams, 172, 174, 175
  of Dominic, 31
  example of, 11
  as Great Dreams, 32-33, 172, 173, 174, 175, 184-185
  little dreams leading to, 137, 143
  of Michael, 161-163
  in other therapies, 77
  as Power Dreams, 172, 173, 174, 175
  readiness for, 31, 53, 81, 82, 89-90, 92, 111, 117, 124, 142
Bright Dreams, 172, 173-174, 175

California, new ideas from, 54
Callahan, Michele, 196
Carole (Lita), 17, 54, 60, 62, 67, 69, 70-75, 78
  dreams of, 72-73, 74-75
  fears of, 70-71

censoring process, 2, 12-13, 36, 49, 117, 129, 142, 159, 160, 175
  secondary processes as, 2, 12
Center for Feeling Therapy, Psychological Corporation, 17, 43, 47, 54, 65, 76, 192-193, 194
  dream explorations at, 54-56
Center Foundation, The, 190-192
  classes of membership in, 191
change:
  of dreams, 68, 124-125
  through dreams, 3, 13, 53, 74-75, 87, 101, 118-125, 129, 131, 139, 163, 176, 184
  little steps for, 118, 137, 176
Clarity:
  of Dream Maker processes, 92, 96-97, 121, 159
  graphing of, 110-112
Clear Dreams, 172, 174, 175
colors, in dreams, 80-81
communities, Dream Maker, 3, 52, 65, 77, 82, 129, 180
Community Training Program (1976), 129-130
connectedness, 81
conscious mind, reaching of, by unconscious, 2, 10, 12, 18-19, 39, 49
conversations, imaginary, 169
Corriere, Richard, see Riggs

Dakota Indians, 46-47
Dancing Elk, 46
"daymares," 2, 147
defenses, 64, 68
Dominic, 17, 18-31, 34-35, 37, 47, 48, 50, 52, 54-56, 62, 64, 67-68, 69, 77, 79, 145, 146
  anxiety of, 20-22, 23-24, 25
  as Werner's helper, 38-45
Don, 177-179

Dream Capabilities Assessment Test (DCAT), 147, 148-156, 189-190
  evaluation of, free, 159
  scoring of, 156, 158-159, 160
Dream Capability Assessment Profile, 157-158, 159
Dream Maker:
  becoming of, 26, 28, 29, 136, 140, 143
  becoming of, in week one, 91-102
  becoming of, in week two, 103-117
  becoming of, in week three, 118-125
  vs. Censor, 12-13, 36, 49, 159, 160, 175
  in childhood, 61, 130, 131
  covert approach of, 24, 40, 48, 60, 84
  creation of dreams by, 26, 27, 42, 60-61, 63, 68, 72, 78, 81-82, 143, 182
  in daytime life, 118, 141, 179
  description and nature of, 24, 26, 50, 51, 52, 125, 141-142
  dreams as secondary to, 26
  existence of, affirmed, 141
  fear of, 2, 45, 51
  having vs. becoming, 135-136
  helpers of, 48, 51, 61-62
  historical appearances of, 1, 50, 136, 181
  nightmares and, 2, 29, 39-40, 48, 130-131, 143
  as person, 12-13, 19, 20, 41-42
  as personal therapist, 142-143
  preparation by, 31, 53, 62, 67, 80, 84, 130, 133, 143, 178, 182
  pursuit by, 20, 27, 28, 39, 43-44, 59-60, 132
  questions about, 141
  recognition of other Dream Makers by, 142

Dream Maker: (cont.)
  responsibility of, 3, 34, 51
  sexual life regained by, 74
  teaching methods of, 61, 62, 64, 80,
    84, 182, 183
Dream Maker Approach, 139, 169,
    185-186, 191, 194, 197
  extension of, 129
  extra-therapeutic uses of, 13
  functional aspects of, 99-100, 103
  Interpretive Approach vs., 164-165
  as nonjudgmental, 96
  one-day workshops in, 130
  rediscovery of, 1, 9-13, 17
Dream Maker Associate Program, 180,
    191, 195-196
Dream Maker Awareness:
  experiencing of, 31, 75
  first step in, 13-14, 53
  meaning of, 2, 117
  for others, 34, 76-78, 81-83
  in other therapies, 77
Dream Maker Group Training, 196-
    197
Dream Maker lectures, 133-134, 194-
    195
Dream Maker Process, 2, 17, 129, 147,
    171
  balance in, 114-115, 124, 146, 175
  changing of, in waking, 91, 98,
    101-102, 117
  dynamics of, 11-12, 83
  graphing of, 103-114
  identifying of, 91-92, 103-117
  interactions in, 97, 159
  live-in programs for, 129
  in other therapies, 77
  risks in, 3
  waiting in, 78
Dream Maker Program, 190-191
Dream Maker programs, 194-197

Dream Maker questions, in exercises,
    94, 105, 107, 111-112, 120, 121,
    122
Dream Maker Tradition, 1-3, 7-14, 17,
    31, 33, 36-37, 45, 77, 124, 143
  healing in, 46-47
  loss of, 32, 36
  meaning of, 2-3
  in modern society, 8
  in other therapies, 77
  regaining of, 33, 65
  sharing of, 3, 34, 37, 125
  stages of, 62, 65
Dream Maker words, 64, 84, 123, 180
Dream Maker workshops, 127-181,
    185, 196
  first meeting of, 135-144
  second meeting of, 145-169
dream questions, in exercises, 93, 95,
    96, 97, 106, 108, 110, 112-113,
    119-120, 121, 122
Dream Research newsletter, 191
Dream Research Project, free evalua-
    tion and scoring from, 158
Dream Retreat, 83
dreams, dreaming:
  active vs. passive, 103-104, 136, 146,
    161, 166, 168
  advice about, 168-169
  of Carole, 72-73, 74-75
  changes accomplished by, 3, 13, 53,
    74-75, 87, 101, 118-125, 129, 131,
    139, 176, 184
  characteristics of, 10, 12, 14, 55,
    80-81, 93, 101, 160, 168, 172, 175
  control of, avoided, 87, 91, 171-173
  of Dominic, 18-20, 24-25, 28, 30-31
  enjoyment of, 80
  feelings and, *see* feelings
  forgetting of, 23, 25, 26, 72, 142,
    164, 167

dreams, dreaming: (cont.)
  of Freud, 35-36
  inventing of, 90, 92, 98
  of Jerry, 63-64, 173-174
  of Joe, 60-61, 69-70, 172-173
  of Lee, 48, 49
  living of, vs. interpreting of, 4, 10,
    11, 35, 50, 79, 84, 87, 90, 99-100,
    101, 117, 160, 164-165
  made-up, 90, 92, 98
  mythic approach to, 13
  of Nakasuk, 56-58
  nightmares and, see nightmares
  past, present, and future connec-
    tions in, 45, 78, 81, 115-117, 125
  as picturing process of feelings,
    101-102, 115, 135, 136, 137, 138,
    139-140, 145, 165, 166-167, 171,
    174, 182
  remembering of, 87-90, 167, 177,
    179
  of Riggs, 23, 59, 78-79, 80-82, 129
  of Steve, 68, 69, 70
  symbolic, see symbolic dreams
  talking about, 31, 83, 89, 90, 97, 162,
    164, 165, 166, 167, 176, 180-181
  of Tarachiwa, 7-8
  teaching about, 7, 31, 34, 53, 61, 62,
    64, 67, 76-78, 80, 81-84, 97, 117,
    127-81, 183
  as transformative, see change
  unifying elements in, 88-89, 96
  waking, 179
  of Werner, 39-40
  as working for or against dreamer,
    13-14, 99-100, 167

educational programs, Dream Maker,
  191, 194-197
Eskimos, 58

exercises (see also body questions;
    Dream Maker questions; dream
    questions; past questions; waking
    questions), 4, 31, 53, 64, 74,
    89-90, 91, 93-98, 101-102, 103-
    116, 119-124, 125, 169
  inventing of, 98
Expression:
  in Dream Maker processes, 92,
    93-94, 119-120, 159
  graphing of, 106-107

Feeling Levels:
  in Bright Dreams, 174
  in Dream Maker processes, 92,
    94-95, 120-121, 159
  graphing of, 108-109
feelings:
  acceptance of, 53, 83, 168
  of body, 72-74
  as completed in dreams, 75, 100-
    102, 146, 175
  as dreams, 35, 90, 94-95, 100, 137,
    139, 145, 165
  in dreams, 4, 10, 12, 42, 43, 68, 80,
    81, 87, 162, 167
  expression of, 12, 20, 31, 51, 71, 87,
    90, 179, 180, 182
  living from, 144, 176, 182, 185
  moods vs., 166-167
  talking about, 31, 90, 162, 164, 165,
    166, 180
  weather reports compared with, 159
  as working for or against dreamer,
    99-100, 140, 167
Feeling Therapy, 191
  unauthorized imitators of, 193
Ferenzi, Sandor, 37
freedom, fear of, 66, 70
Freud, Sigmund, 12, 35-37, 50, 177,
  195

friends:
  advice to and from, 31
  help from, in dreams, 168
  talking to, about dreams, 31, 83, 89, 90, 97, 164, 165, 166, 167, 176, 180-181
Functional School of Psychotherapy, 192

Gestalt therapy, 77
*Going Sane*, 129
"Going Sane and the Breakthru Dream" (lecture), 194-195
Good Eagle, 46
Great Dreams, 32-33, 172, 173, 174, 175, 184-185
Greeks, ancient, 50

Hart, Joseph, *see* Joe
Hillman, James, 65
hyperactivity, 115
hysteria, 114

Indians, 7-8, 19, 26, 36-37, 46-47, 50, 52, 91, 181
information sources, 194-197
"insearch," 3
intellectualizations, 114
interpersonal relations, improvement of, 53
interpretation of dreams, *see* dreams, dreaming
Iroquois Indians, 7-8, 19, 181

Jerry (Jerry Binder), 17, 54-55, 60, 62-64, 65, 67-68, 78, 175, 177-179, 180, 196
  anger of, 62-63
  dreams of, 63, 173-174
  as Steve's helper, 68-69
  as workshop leader, 136, 142, 145, 147, 159, 160, 172

Joe (Joseph Hart), 17, 52, 54-56, 58-62, 63, 64, 66, 78, 79-80, 81, 82, 174, 175
  anxiety of, 53
  as Carole's helper, 72-74
  dreams of, 60-61, 69-70, 172-173
  as workshop leader, 136, 139-140, 143-144, 145, 146, 160-163, 164, 165, 171
Judy, 130, 131-181, 183-185
  Great Dream of, 184-185
  Michael's relationship with, 132-133, 143, 145, 183
  in workshop group, 136-139, 145-146, 160, 176, 180-181
Jung, Carl, 35-37, 50, 195
Jungian analysis, 65, 77

Karle, Werner, *see* Werner

Lee (Lee Woldenberg), 3, 17, 47-52, 55-56, 62, 63, 64, 67-68, 69, 72, 77, 78, 174, 189
  anxiety of, 47-51
  dreams of, 48, 49, 51
  father of, 49-50
  as workshop leader, 136, 145, 164, 165
life crises, 7, 28, 30, 35, 132
life pictures, dream pictures related to, 175
life scenes, in workshop study, 175
life span, 182
life-style, life time vs., 182
light, as waking alarm, 89
limits, in dreams, 168, 172
Lita, *see* Carole
Los Angeles, changes in, 76
LSD trips, 2, 47, 60

made-up dreams, 90, 92, 98
made-up exercises, 98

Make-It-Work Technique, 145, 161
  six steps of, 163
Michael, 130-181, 183-185
  Judy's relationship with, 131-133,
    176-177, 183
  in workshop group, 139-144, 145-
    146, 160-163, 176, 180-181
moodiness, 115, 165-166

Nakasuk, dream of, 56-58
nightmares, 2, 13, 29, 39-40, 48, 69,
  130-131, 143, 171
normality, Dream Maker breakthrough of, 27

past questions, in exercises, graphing
  of, 104-105, 106-107, 109, 111
peak experiences, 2
picturing process, in dreams, 101-102,
  115, 135, 136, 137, 138, 139-140,
  145, 165, 166-167, 171, 174, 182
Power Dreams, 172, 173, 174, 175
psychoanalytic theory, 12, 55, 77,
  99-100
psychophysiological research, 191
psychotherapists, as patients, 9, 37
publications, Dream Maker, 191

Reality, awareness of, after Breakthru
  Dream, 31, 34
recording:
  of day's activities, 89
  of exercise answers, 91
Riggs (Richard Corriere), 17, 37, 48,
  50, 52, 53, 55, 59-61, 63, 64,
  67-68, 76-84, 174, 175, 176, 197
  as Dominic's helper, 21-22, 23-24,
    26, 30, 34
  Dream Maker research of, 39, 47,
    52, 76-77
  dreams of, 23, 59, 78-79, 80-82, 129

Riggs   (Richard   Corriere):   (cont.)
  as Joe's helper, 59-61
  as workshop leader, 136-139, 142-
    144, 145, 159, 163, 165, 172
Role:
  in Dream Maker processes, 92, 93,
    119, 159
  graphing of, 103-105

Satori, 2, 52, 55, 111
Senoi (Malaysia), 31-33, 50, 61
  as "Dream people," 32, 33, 181
sexuality, 74, 98, 132, 138, 176-177
shamanism, 7, 8, 55, 58
sounds, in dreams, 93
Steve, 17, 54, 62, 65-70, 78, 145, 146
  dreams of, 68, 69, 70
  fears of freedom in, 66, 70
symbolic dreams:
  balance in, 115
  as malfunctioning, 146
  release from, 11, 12, 14, 34, 101,
    117, 160

talking:
  about day's activities, 90
  about dreams, see dreams
  about feelings, 31, 90, 162, 164, 165,
    166, 180
Tarachiwa, 7-8, 34
teaching (see also Dream Maker lec-
    tures; Dream Maker programs;
    Dream Maker workshops):
  Dream Maker methods of, 61, 62,
    64, 80, 84, 182, 183
  about dreams, see dreams
  through feelings, 88
therapy:
  at Center for Feeling Therapy, 192
  in Dream Maker Tradition, 77
  dreams as addition to, 55
  dreams intensified in, 53

time, distortion of, 22, 23
"touch," as Dream Maker word, 180
*Transformation of Dreams, The,* 3, 192

unconscious, breaking through to, 2, 10, 18-19, 39, 49

waking experience:
  activity vs. passivity in, 120
  advice for, 168-169
  consequences of dreams in, 3, 34, 51-52, 90, 91, 98, 101-102, 117, 161, 176, 185
  Dream Maker Process graphed in, 113, 114

waking experience: (cont.)
  picturing of, 115, 118
  pretrial of dream methods in, 118
  symbolism in, 101
waking questions, in exercises, 4, 93, 94, 95, 96, 97-98, 101, 105, 107, 109, 111, 116, 119, 120, 121, 122
Werner (Werner Karle), 3, 17, 37, 38-45, 47, 50, 56, 62, 64, 67, 77, 191
  anxiety of, 39-44
  dreams of, 39-40, 41-42, 44
  as Lee's helper, 48-51
wish fulfillment, 12
Woldenberg, Lee, *see* Lee